Dedicated

To The

Hip-Hop

Generation

FROM POVERTY
TO
POWER MOVES

The True Story

DASHAWN TAYLOR

with Stephanie Johnson

NEW YORK   LOS ANGELES   ATLANTA   LONDON

This publication is designed to provide competent and reliable information regarding the subject matter covered. However, it is sold with the understanding that the author and the publisher are not engaged in rendering legal, financial or other professional advice. Laws and practices often vary from state to state and if legal or other expert assistance is required, the services of a professional should be sought. The author and publisher specifically disclaim any liability that is incurred from the use or application of the contents of this book.

Although based on a true story, certain events in the book have been fictionalized for educational content and impact.

Next Level Publishing
PO Box 83
Newark, NJ 07101

From Poverty To Power Moves

ISBN (10)   0-9800154-1-3
ISBN (13)   978-0-9800154-1-6

Manufactured in the United States of America

Cover Photo By: Azza Suliman (azza_suliman@yahoo.co.uk)
Creative Design: Ultimate Media Design Studio
Special Guest Editor: Cynthia Anderson
Cover Fashion Provided By: RH2 Apparel, CrossoverWatches.Com
For more info and copies log onto www.nextlevelpublishing.com

ACKNOWLEDGEMENTS

Acknowledgements are always hard for me. And it's not because I don't like to give thanks, it's just that there has been so many people that came into my life that inspired me to do better. The following acknowledgments are in no way in order of importance. If you find yourself at the end of the list or omitted, blame it on my mind and not my heart.

To the most important WOMAN in my life -

Gave me life! Gave me strength! And gave me a reason to grind the way I do! My Mother is by far the most important person in my life. Raising four boys in the hood? What more can I say? You'll never have to want for anything as long as there is breath in my lungs. I Love You Mother!

To the most important MAN in my life -

I wouldn't have the courage or the "audacity" to be somebody if it wasn't for this man. It's crazy because I use to think that I was just born with this "drive" to be somebody and all this time it was my Father that put the "bug" in my ear when I was just a few weeks old. So pops, what can I say? Thanks! Love you for real!

To my Brothers -

Michael, Steven and Charles. Only "we" know exactly what we went through as kids to survive. Although we all went our separate ways at one point in life, I always knew that we could find a way to get money together. Trust me, "Joanne's" boys will make something big happen. Just a matter of time. Michael- just "calm down" and let the game come to you. You'll know when to strike when you see the opening. Steve-you got too much talent and "game" to go out like that. Wherever you are, get money and keep it gangsta. Charles aka DJ Symphony – you got the most talent and creativity out of all of us. Just stay focus and don't let the world tell you how to get it. Remember, I got ya back!

To my Extended Family -

My brother Brian. I know you got your "flowing skills" up. But keep it versatile. You got more "skills" than you think. Just don't spit lyrics…..own them too! To my sisters Alikah and Bria you know I love you guys to death. Stay focus and make your mother and father proud one day.

To my Bloodline -

My Grandparents Ruth Taylor and Benny Taylor (R.I.P.) (Sorry about the photos) and Rosetta Smith and Horace Smith (R.I.P. – we miss you so much). To my uncles: Uncle Kenny (my silent inspiration), Uncle John (my "get money" inspiration), Uncle Herbert, Uncle Roosevelt, Uncle Leonard, Uncle Junior. To my aunts: Aunt Cynt (my favorite aunt), Aunt Marie, Aunt Stella, Aunt Pat, Aunt Dorothy, Aunt Ronia (R.I.P.), Great Aunt Tee (R.I.P.), Aunt Mary O'Bannion and Uncle Richard O'Bannion. To my cousins: Simone, Stephanie, Tawanda, Chucky, Nicole, Cookie, Pam, Sabania, Eric, Terrel, Dwayne, Aunt Peaches, Uncle Curtis, Aunt Betsy (R.I.P.), Cousin Dorothy, Mark (Salaadin) Kinslow, Anthony Kinslow, Kisha, Darnella, Kitty,

Lena, Larry, Dennis, Junior McClinton, Anthony Mclinton, Reese McClinton and Alvin aka Neph Dolo and to my beautiful niece Harmony.

To The Extended NPS Family -

Michael Green (General Mike), Charles Walker (Jah Shamel), Cheron Lewis (Babylee), Semaj (Freedom God), Aaron (Shabazz), E-Power, Sunstar, Wilbur King, Kevin Robinson (DJ Kashif R.I.P.), DJ Juice, Cortez Phillips, Byron Phillips, Kevin Hall, Wayne Hall, Darryle Hall, Dashon Williams (Smurf), Black Prince, Dramatic, Tim, Rasun, Calvin, James & Rodney Bowlin.

The Real-Hiphop.Com Staff -

Kyle "New" Newsome – they don't even know what is about to hit 'em. 12 years deep and we still didn't miss a beat! I smell a dynasty coming, let's make it happen!
DJ Muhammad – no turning back now. Remember if it don't make dollars then it don't make sense!
J-Mil – Don't drop the ball my nigga. You are on the launching pad.
Felicia Newsome – the real brains behind the brawn!

(Damn, look how light we got! Just goes to show that you must have something "extra" to be down.)

RH2 Disciples (Guilty By Association) -

Carl Cole (CFC), Cynthia Strickland (Cee Cee Personalized), Akilah Horton, Samar Newsome (I need to hear that debut album....make it happen!), L.S. (You taught me the real meaning of sacrifice), Ahmed Muhammad (Thanks for the belief), D'Erica (thanks for all the help...but it's not over), Richard "Younglord" Frierson, Sire Steeleheart, Reginald Alcindor, Chester Tatmon, Antionette Bennet, Isadora Douglas, Vic Battle, Craig Newsome, Jamil Cobb, Club M-15 (Nick and Celleste), Spark, Johnny Wise and Unique, Crossover Watches, NBANFL.Com, Jenna & Robby Zumsteg (Cameo Cast), Christian, Brad, Angel, Lily.

Martinique "Butta" Moore (now the world gets to see what we have known for mad years), Craig "NewBomb" Newsome, Charlie "Rock" Newsome (R.I.P.), Daniel Valcourt, Antoinette Bennett, Mama Newsome, Aunt Sharon, Uncle Fred, My Cousin Third, Kristen, Laz, Jeri Middlebrook, Salisha Adams, Greg, Jason "J-O" Owens, Antonique, Pro-Tim, Alan McGriff, Ed Wilson & Pat Wilson (GYM), Latrice Burnette (Atlantic Records), John Bartleson (Def Jam), Loose Canon, Melky Jean, Eric Brewer (Rhema), Ezra and Dallas Johnson, Janiel, Gadget, Haslyn, Mega, Larry "Lak" Henderson, The Thorobredz, T'wana Denard, Melinda McKenzi, Calvin Berry (Vertex), Rob Cole, Sheya Blackwell, Tahisha, Alicia, Malkia Murry, Ralph Burgess, Dion, Echo Hattix. DC Bookman, Tiah, Treasure E. Blue and IDC.

Hakeem and Mad Linx, Wendy Williams, DJ Kay Slay, Toya, Sunny, Megatron, Big Boi, John Blassingame, Latia Palmer, Melissa Bonnick (Music Vision), Shante, Pezo and Bird (Hot 102VA), Murad Muhammad, Mujtaaba, Nija, Wina, O and Papoose (good luck with your career dog), Patrick Laguire, Ruby (Sly Magazine), Shara, Tash Mahogany, Tee-Cookies, Deborah Lanier, Tiny, Whip.

My R.U. Family -

George White, Mikah Johnson, Ibrihim, Dean Plummer, Dean Smith, Hester Stephenson, Charles Jones, Jamaal Phillips, Seon, Bobby, Dax, Maurice Leftwich, Rad, Ramik, Sam, Altareek, Felix, Eugene Robinson, Brian, Earl, Brock, Tynaah, Bill Bradley, Rena, Shaniqua, The Africana House, Jermaine, Anzel, Rosey, Mike, The Paul Robeson Floor, Tasha, The Wu, The Whole Shorty Crew, LedLak, Rabu, Sabu.

To Hip-Hop -

2 Live Crew,3rd Bass, 50 Cent , 69 Boys, Above the Law, Afrika Bambaataa and the Zulu Nation, Afu-Ra, The Alchemist, Tha Alkaholiks , AMG, Amil-lion, Kool Keith, Ice T, Angie Martinez, Antoinette, Arrested Development, Baby Bash, Beanie Sigel, Beastie Boys, Beatnuts, Big Daddy Kane, Big L (R.I.P.), Big Punisher (R.I.P.), Biz Markie, Black Eyed Peas, Black Star (Mos Def, Talib Kweli), Bobby Brown, Bone Thugs n Harmony,

Bonecrusher, Boo-Yaa T.R.I.B.E., Boss, Bow Wow, Bubba Sparxxx, Busta Rhymes, Bumpy Knuckles, Camoflauge (R.I.P.), Cam'ron, Canibus, Cappadonna, Cassidy, Chingy, Chubb Rock, Clipse (Pusha T, Malice), CNN (Capone-N-Noreaga), The Cold Crush Brothers, DJ Tony Tone, Grandmaster Caz, Common, Company Flow, Compton's Most Wanted (MC Eiht, Tha Chill, DJ Slip, DJ Mike T), Cool C, Coolio The Coup, Crash Crew, C-Rayz-Walz, Crooked I, Cash Money Records, Cypress Hill (B Real, Muggs, Sen Dog, Eric Bobo), D Block, Royce Da 5'9", D12 (Bizarre, Bugz –R.I.P., Eminem, Kon Artis, Kuniva, Proof, Swift), Daddy Yankee, Da Brat, Das Efx, Daz Dillinger, D.T.I.C., De La Soul (Pasemaster Mase, Posdnuos, Trugoy the Dove), Dead Prez (Sticman, M-1), Deceptikonz , Damon Dash, Del tha Funkee Homosapien, Digital Underground, Dilated Peoples, DJ Jazzy Jeff, DJ KaySlay, DJ Symphony, DJ P-Cutta, Dipset (Cam'ron, Hell Rell, Jimmy Jones, Juelz Santana, 40 Cal, Duke Da God, Freaky Zeeky), DJ Big Mike, DJ Doughboy, DJ Green Latern, DJ Kool Herc, DJ Clue, Megatron, DJ Storm, DJ Enuff, DJ Quik, DJ Screw (R.I.P.), DJ Shadow, DJ Yulian, DJ Threat (R.I.P.), DJ Justo Faison (R.I.P.), DMX, Domino, The_D.O.C. Dr. Dre, Drag-On, Dungeon Family, E-40, The East Side Boyz, Tha Eastsidaz, Ed O.G, Eightball & MJG, EPMD (Erick Sermon, PMD, DJ_Scratch), Eric B, Eve, Everlast.

Fabolous , The Fat Boys, Fat Joe, Fatman Scoop, Flipmode Squad, Floetry, Foxy Brown, Fredro Starr, Freeway, Fresh Prince, Funkmaster Flex, The Fugees (Lauryn Hill, Pras Michel, Wyclef Jean), Funky Four Plus One, Grafh, G-Dep, G-Unit (50 Cent, Lloyd Banks, Tony Yayo, Young Buck, Spider Loc, Olivia, The Game),Gang Starr (DJ Premier, Guru), The Geto Boys, Irv Gotti, Grandmaster Flash, Guerilla Black, Heavy D and the Boyz, House of Pain, Hi-Tek, Ice Cube, Ice-T, Immortal Technique , Insane Clown Posse, Allen Iverson.

J-Kwon, Ja Rule, Jacki-O, Jadakiss, Jay-Z, Jayo Felony, Jaz-O, Jean Grae, Jermaine Dupri, Jeru The Damaja, Joe Budden, John Cena, JT Money, Juelz Santana, Jungle Brothers, Jurassic 5, Juvenile, Kanye West, Kid Rock, Killer Mike, King T, Knoc-turn'al, Kokane, Kanye West, Kool G Rap, KRS One, Kurtis Blow, Kurupt, Kwamé, La Familia, Lady of Rage, Lil' Flip, Lil Jon and The Eastside Boyz, Lil Kim, Lil' Mo, Lil' Romeo, Lil Wayne, Lil'

Scrappy, Lil' Troy, Lil' Zane, Lisa "Left Eye" Lopes (R.I.P.), Little Brother, LL Cool J, Loon, Lord Finesse, Lords of the Underground, Lovebug Starski, The Lox (Jadakiss, Styles P, Sheek Luchiano), Ludacris, Mad Rapper, Magoo, Main Source, Marky Mark (aka Mark Wahlberg), Marley Marl, Mase, Maino, Master Ace, Master P, MC Breed, MC Hammer, MC Lyte, MC Ren, MC Shan, McGruff , Mike Jones, Missy Elliott, Mobb Deep, Monie Love, M.O.P, Mos Def, Ms. Jade, Mystikal, Napoleon, The Nappy Roots, Nas (a.k.a. Nasir Jones), Native Tongues Posse, Naughty By Nature, Nick Cannon , Notorious B.I.G. (R.I.P.), N.W.A. (DJ Yella, Dr. Dre, Eazy-E (R.I.P.), Ice Cube, MC Ren), Obie Trice, O.C., Onyx, OutKast (André 3000, Big Boi), Outlawz (Tupac Shakur (R.I.P.), EDI, Kadafi (R.I.P.), Kastro, Fatal), The Outsidaz (Young Zee, Pace Won, Dee You, Rah Digga, Eminem, Azizz, DJ Muhammed, Slang Ton (R.I.P.), Loon One, Dentyne, Yah Lova, DJ Mudd, Venton, Bizarre, Hostile, Axe, & NawShis).

Papoose Puff Daddy, Panjabi MC, The Pharcyde, Pharoahe Monch, Poor Righteous Teachers, Prince Paul, Professor Griff, Public Enemy (Chuck D, Flavor Flav, Terminator X), Quan, Queen Latifah, Queen Pen, Rah Digga, Russell Simmons, Rakim, Rasco, Ras Kass, Red Café, Redman, The Roots, Roxanne Shante, Ruff Ryders (DMX, Flashy, L.O.X., Drag-On, Eve, Swizz Beatz , Kartoon), Rufus Blaq, Run-DMC (DMC, Jam Master Jay (R.I.P), Run), Schoolly D, Shawnna, Silkk The Shocker, Sir Mix-A-Lot, Skillz, Sleepy Brown, Slick Rick, Slim Thug, Sly Boogy, Smoothe the Hustler, Trigger the Gambler, Soulja Slim (R.I.P.), Special Ed, Murphy Lee, Nelly, Sticky Fingaz, The Sugarhill Gang, Suge Knight, Terror Squad (Fat Joe, Big Pun (R.I.P.), Cuban Link, Armageddon, Triple Seis, Tony Sunshine, Remy Martin), Tha Dogg Pound, Three 6 Mafia, Timberland, A Tribe Called Quest, Tonedeff, Tony Touch, Too Short, Treacherous Three (Kool Moe Dee, Special K, DJ Easy Lee), Trick Daddy, Triple 6 Mafia, Trina, C-Murder, Master P, Twista, UGK, Bun B, Pimp C, Ultramagnetic MCs, UNLV, U.T.F.O., Vanilla Ice, Wu-Tang Clan (Ghostface Killah, GZA, Inspectah Deck, Masta Killa, Method Man, Ol' Dirty Bastard (R.I.P.), Raekwon, RZA, U-God), Xzibit, Ying Yang Twins, Young Jeezy, Young MC, Young Zee, YoYo, YZ. If you are not on this list, please don't take it personal!

CONTENTS

ForeWord

by Stephanie Johnson

When I was first offered the challenge to write Dashawn's story, I was intimidated by the main focus: Hip Hop. I was nervous and unsure that I could translate his feelings so that you, the reader, could feel them as he intended.

As I wove the story of a young boy who was lead by words harmonized by, at that time, complete strangers to him in the Hip Hop world, I began to understand Dashawn's focus and slowly but surely was able to appreciate his passion; his desire to be more than just an element in the Hip Hop world. It opened up a window that before participating in this project was cracked here and there because I just didn't get it. (I know you're laughing and that's ok!).

I didn't know how Hip Hop could engulf the mind, and if you're open enough, change the way you think, by telling the real deal. Shattering many myths that we were taught as children, Hip Hop is a reality, Dashawn's reality and now mine.

DT,

Thank you so much for allowing me to enter your world. Thank you for broadening my horizons by explaining to me in humble words your world as no one ever knew it. Thank you for teaching me that it's not all about smooth words of song that tug at my heart and that the harsh reality of Hip Hop is just as real and heartbreaking. I'm proud to have been at your side in this endeavor.

Until the next time,

Stephanie A. F. Johnson, Author
She's Got Issues, Rockin Robin
Co-Author From Poverty to Power Moves
www.safjohnson.com

1
The Promise

It was the first time I ever saw a gun. I saw a few guns on television before but I never saw one like this and in this manner. It was pointed directly in my face. The barrel was about two feet away, but it felt like it was two inches from my face.

"Make a damn sound and it's over!"

I couldn't see his face at all because he had a sweat hood on that was pulled tight to his face. But I could tell that he was serious by the tone of his voice. See, the mood of the whole situation had changed. One minute we were going to the store to buy some groceries and the next minute we were being robbed. I put my hands up. I didn't know if that was the right thing to do, I just did it. I was only five years old and getting robbed at gunpoint with my older brothers. My oldest brother Michael, who was only 10 at the time, looked towards me. I saw that he was scared and he quickly put his hands up. My second eldest brother Steven was 8 at the time and he followed suit, putting his hands up too.

"Give me whatever you got!"

Mike quickly went into his pocket and gave up the money. Five dollars, that's all we had. The guy took the money and ran off. Scared and confused we simply ran back home. My father was so pissed that he went outside to look for the guy but he was long gone. That was the first time I ever had a gun pointed at me, but it wouldn't be the last.

Trenton, New Jersey is a hard city. Currently, its total population is 85,000 with an unemployment rate of 12 percent. The national crime index for the United States is 330. Trenton has a crime index of 785.8; nearly doubling the national average. 21 percent of the city's population lives below the poverty level. Trenton has over 10 elementary schools, 5 middle schools and 1 high school.

As a child I grew up poor. There were other kids in my neighborhood that grew up in worse circumstances than I did. But for the most part, we all shared a life of poverty and stress. I spent the first 18 years of my life trying to escape this city. For as long as I can remember, I wanted to get as far away from this place as I could. I've always imagined Trenton as a trap for me. I cringed at the very thought of living here the rest of my life. When I was in the first grade I made a promise to myself that I would do everything that I could to make it out of this place alive and be somebody. The road to escape Trenton was long and rough. This is my story.

2
14 Hampton Avenue

I was born and raised in Trenton. For the first few years of my life I lived primarily on the west side of town. It wasn't bad living in that section when I was coming up. Although I was aware that we were living in the 'hood and we were broke most of the time, we still managed to have fun and make a way to enjoy our lives. And by "we" I am speaking of my three brothers and our close friends. Growing up poor was a serious learning experience. It was tough and frustrating at times because as I got older I wanted to do more and wanted to have more things. I always thought about the future and thought big. Thinking about what I was going to do when I got older took my mind off of my situation at the time. It was an escape.

Because of the amount of people who lived in our house, some days we'd eat less than we wanted to. Christmas and birthdays would pass and we would make do. It was frustrating at the time and that made me more determined to make a better way for myself. I knew it wasn't always going to be like this and as a child I had no idea *what* would be my saving grace. All I knew was that something big was going to happen and *I* was going to be the one to make it happen. As a child, I would have dreams of being a firefighter, a wrestler, an auto mechanic, a bus driver, the president, an artist and even a preacher. And despite the fact that I couldn't make my mind up about which way to go, I was full of determination and I knew for sure that I wanted out of the ghetto.

During the earlier part of my life, my father was around. I didn't live the stereotypical life where I didn't know who he was. And up until I was about 14, he was a constant member of my family. When my father was around, he ran a tight ship. He made sure we obeyed my mother, did some work around the house and had good personal hygiene. I noticed in a lot of my childhood pictures, I was dressed in suits. He encouraged that and wanted us to do well academically and morally. I mean, with four boys he had to be overbearing. He wanted us to succeed and wanted us to do better than he did. He didn't want us to repeat the mistakes that he made like getting into trouble and having kids. It sounds ironic, I know, but it's the truth.

We moved a lot when I was young. In fact, I went to six different elementary schools. That was rough because I had to meet new friends and start all over at every school. Most kids didn't welcome us to the new neighborhood without a good fist fight, so needless to say, every time my mother told us that we were moving we had to get prepared to keep our guard up. But growing up with three brothers helped out a lot because we were rarely alone. One move in particular proved to shape a major part of my personality.

In the middle of third grade I remember going home early from school one day. My mother pulled us out of school and brought us all home. There were a few boxes already packed and she told us to get our things together. To this day, I never asked my mother why we were moving. Over the next two days she told us to make sure we packed everything up and cleaned the floors and the windows. We moved a few times before this one, but I could tell that this one was different. The prior moves were to larger apartments. But this time we were moving with my grandmother. We were going to live with my maternal grandmother and my father wasn't coming with us. My grandmother lived in the Wilbur Section of Trenton. This was by far the worst part of Trenton at the time. We visited my grandmother a few times while we lived on the west side and we hated it. The kids in the neighborhood were rougher than the west side and we didn't have many friends. The only kids we knew before we actually moved there were three brothers that lived a few houses down from my grandmother. Marlon, Michael and Corey Green were our only friends in Wilbur section. My mother would take us to our grandmother's house every few months or so and we would play with the "Green Boys" down the street. It was always fun because we didn't have to go too far from the house and they were cool. I remember when we would come over and they were not there; we would be so bored. But now we were moving in the neighborhood for good. We moved into my grandmother's house where two of my uncles and two of my aunts were staying with their children. My grandmother and grandfather were also there and now my mother was moving in with her four boys. Things were really tight at my grandmother's house. We stayed with her for two years. Two very long years that would prove to play a crucial part in my life.

Friendship

I can still remember the first night that we stayed at my grandmother's house. My mother made us unpack all of our clothes and setup our room. The first few months, my brothers and I all stayed in the attic together. I remember feeling really scared because I knew that we would have to start a new school the following day. My older brothers were already in middle school and it would be my younger brother and I that would head out to the neighborhood grade school the next day. Mike Green already told me about the problems that he had in the school and I automatically assumed that I would be fighting everyday just to get home. I stayed up later than everybody else that night. Like any typical child, I kept playing all the worst scenarios in my head over and over again until I fell asleep.

My mother woke up extremely early that morning because she had to make her way to work, which now was close to an hour away. By the time we woke up to get ready for school she was already gone. We tried to go through the normal routine of getting ready for school but it wasn't the same without my mother there. My grandmother made breakfast and we ate slowly before we headed out to school. The first walk to school was a breeze because my uncle walked my little brother and me down the street. I took notice of how long the walk was and calculated how long the *run* would be.

Once we got to the school we had to report straight to the main office to fill out paperwork. I remember looking at the kids and trying to figure out which one was going to be the problem for me. But before I could get a few good looks, the assistant principal came into the office and told my brother and me to follow him. He walked us down the main halls until we came to my brother's classroom. He told my brother that this was his new class and instructed him to go inside the classroom. The assistant principal turned back to me and we continued to my class. I kept thinking to myself that I would soon bump into one of those "bad kids". As we got closer to the end of the hall, the assistant principal began to slow down and told me that my class was the next door. He opened the door for me and I walked in. I remember my heart pounding like a bass drum. I was so busy scanning the faces in the room that I didn't even hear the teacher tell me to come to the front of the class. As I was scanning the room I saw a familiar face staring right back at me. Mike Green. Yes! My neighborhood friend was in the same class as me and I was excited. At that exact moment I regained my ability to hear and I could hear the teacher instructing me to come to the front of the room. I was all smiles.

Having a friend in my school and especially in my class helped me adjust to my new surroundings. Mike Green and I stuck together and helped each other a lot. When it came to school work, lunch money or problems with other kids, we basically stayed tight and gave each other a hand when we needed it. School to me became a way to get out. I never disliked school and although I wasn't getting crazy good grades in the beginning, I used it as a way to talk to other kids and socialize. I was never shy or ever in a situation where I was uncomfortable talking to people. When I moved to the 4th grade I started taking school seriously despite the fact that I had an attention span problem. I wasn't diagnosed with Attention Deficit Disorder but it was very difficult for the teachers to hold my interest for very long. I probably should've been paying more attention but I would doodle and draw pictures instead of listening to the lesson that was being taught. Sitting still and concentrating on the lesson was "not me". The ironic thing was that I still got good grades. But during those first couple of months at my grandmother's house, I did not want to be there. I couldn't wait to get to school and get away from there. The summers were even worse. We would spend a lot of days playing in the park, getting into trouble around the house, or playing football in the street. But for the most part I really didn't look forward to much as a child besides going to school and playing away from the house.

My First Hustle

Growing up in Wilbur Section was rough and full of poverty. Anything I could do to get money, I tried. Of course getting money from my family was tough because it wasn't much to go around. If I got good grades, I remember I would get a few bucks from my uncles. My older brother had a paper route and he would give us some change from his route if we helped him out. But as a kid with a sweet tooth, I needed more.

There was a lady that lived around the corner from me and I can really only refer to her as Miss Toni. She lived on East State Street and I used to be cool with her son. Miss Toni had a really filthy house. I remembered it because no one wanted to go over there. She would have clothes everywhere and a lot of dishes in the sink. I believe only she and her three children lived there. I'm not sure how it started but her son and I used to clean up a lot when I was over there. He would ask her for money right after we finished and she would give us a dollar to split. One day I was walking by her house from school by myself and she told me to come on the porch. She asked me if I wanted to clean her house. The first time she approached me felt weird but she said that she would pay me to do it. Her method of paying us was with food stamps. She gave me two $1 food stamps to clean her house. Now, although we were broke at my grandmother's house, we still had actual cash. This was the first time I had seen a food stamp. But I figured that they spend just as good as cash so I agreed. I cleaned the house and took the money home.

I didn't know where to spend the food stamps, so I talked to my older brother about it. He knew exactly what they were. He took them from me and bought some candy. From that day, I would go over to her house, which seemed to get worse every time. I'd clean the house, wash the dishes, and toss the clothes, for example. Now remember, I was young and most of the time I wasn't even supposed to *be* around the corner but I would go over there anyway. Some days I would go there and there would be so many dishes in her house, that it overwhelmed me. But I would sit there and make it happen. She gave me $1 and $5 food stamps. To me that was a hustle.

One time I just went over there because I was going on a trip to the Philadelphia Zoo. I was 9 years old and in the fourth grade. There was this turkey hoagie at a local store that I loved, and that's what I wanted to take with me on my trip. So I went over to her house one Sunday and asked her what she needed me to do. She told me that she didn't really have a lot of money but there were a few dishes that needed to be cleaned. She also wanted me to clean her backyard. She led me to her backyard, which had soda cans, garbage bags, cardboard boxes, old pots and a lot of garbage. I cleaned for 4 hours straight and she gave me $3. I didn't like that at all, so I came back and reminded her of what I'd just done. I asked for $5 as payment. She gave it to me. That was my first negotiation and I used that $5 for my trip.

I never cleaned her house after that day. I felt uneasy going to her house without her son around because it felt like she was taking advantage of me. I learned a lot from the situation. I realized then that my family was not as poor as some other families in the neighborhood. And although we had all of these people living under one roof, we were never on food stamps or public assistance. For me to take food stamps as payment for odd jobs was crazy. I wasn't ashamed because it was what it was. Even as I got older, my friends and people I knew were on welfare and I understood the whole concept of just letting people live and not stressing them out. Circumstances are sometimes beyond our control and are sometimes unfortunate.

Boiling Point

For nearly two years, my mother and her four boys held on while the mounting pressures of living with the entire family began to build. Drug abuse, poverty, police brutality and chaos were all around us. We were getting into more fights with the kids from around the corner and our neighbor was even shot and killed over a drug deal. My mother definitely wanted more for us. A few months before we moved out of my grandmother's house, a crazy situation happened that forced my parents to make a serious change in our living situation. I was about nine at the time and in the middle of the fifth grade.
Like every typical night in Wilbur section, at around seven, all the kids would come in the house, eat, take our baths and were *then* allowed to watch TV with my grandfather. We had leftovers most of the time. We had things like soup with neck bones, pig's feet, chitlins, deer and I even had turtle a few times. I really didn't want to eat like that, but I understood that my mother and my grandparents were doing the best they could for us. My brothers and my three

cousins always complained about it. We would even race to see who could finish first so we could get it over with.

One particular night, I finished dinner first. As a house rule, we would have to eat at the table, all the kids at once, and when we were done we washed our hands and were permitted to watch TV. I was watching Dukes of Hazards on this particular night. It was around 8:00 and I was sitting in the living room on the floor with my brothers, aunts and my mother. I remember sitting there looking at the table and hearing a small noise outside. For some strange reason I looked at the window. All of a sudden I heard a loud crash. I saw the curtain flow toward me. I heard my mother scream and my grandmother ran in my direction. The sound was so damn loud. It almost felt like whatever was under the curtain was coming straight towards me. Everybody started running and I remember my cousins running downstairs and we ran upstairs. I can't remember what I was thinking at the time but I do remember just having a bad feeling come over me. Somebody had thrown a huge brick through our window and it fell right in the center of our living room. My uncles ran out the door amidst the huge commotion that was going on outside.

Now at nine years old, I am thinking that everything is happening at once. I'm thinking every scary movie that I have ever watched is coming true. It felt like I wasn't going to make it. I could hear my grandfather and uncles outside and apparently some people were fighting with my aunt. We're all still upstairs, my cousins were crying. And then there's me shaking in the corner; shaking compulsively. This was a traumatic experience for me at nine years old. Looking back today, it saddens me that I was so young and had to go through, what seemed at the time, such a devastating moment. My mother was considerably upset and attempted to calm me down. It took a moment to calm me down and I was finally all right. But the memory will always stay with me. Something drastic must have happened with my mother's situation because not long after the brick occurrence, my mother got an apartment in the Mill Hill section of Trenton. She and my father were back together and we packed up our things and moved from 14 Hampton Avenue.

3
The Martin House

During the early 80's, crack cocaine made its way down to Trenton and hit the city in astronomical proportions. Drugs and violence became a strong force around the neighborhoods in the city and the streets became worse and worse. My mother didn't want us to play in the streets too much so she decided to enroll us in different after school programs and summer camps to keep us busy. Before leaving 14 Hampton Avenue, my mother signed us up for an after school program that was right down the street from my grandmother's house. It was called the Martin House.

I remember my first day going to the Martin House. I was still living with my grandmother at the time. I was in the fifth grade and my mother told us to head down to the after school program instead of coming back home from school. When I arrived at the building I didn't know if it was the right place.

Most of the houses on the street were rundown and some were even abandoned. When I got to the house it looked like every other house on the block. I realized I was in the right place because of a sign on the door that read Martin House. Before I could open the door, this tall, skinny, middle-aged white man greeted me. He was smiling at me and invited me inside. He introduced himself as Father Bill. Before I could tell him my name he said that he already knew me. My brother Michael was already attending the program and my mother told them that she was going to eventually send all of us down there.

When I came into the house it initially looked like a regular house. But then Father Bill took me on a tour and I quickly noticed that this was no ordinary house. On the first floor there was a huge Chapel on the left side of the house. They used this room to hold prayer services and sometimes conduct meetings. As you moved into the right side of the building there was a small nursery for the younger kids. Going towards the back of the house there was a clothing store similar to the Salvation Army. The Martin House would take clothes and other items as donations and sell them back to the community at very low prices. The back of the Martin House was used for the older kids and the Boy Scouts. After touring the house, I was instructed to complete my homework and told that a counselor would help me make sure it was correct. Ironically, the counselors were older kids from the neighborhood. The Martin House employed kids from the ages of 15-18 to help monitor the younger kids and teach them new things.

As it turns out, the Martin House Community Center was started by two priests, Father Bill and

Father Brian in 1978. Its purpose was to help rebuild Trenton. Instead of holding church services and preaching the Word of God, they were more into hearing the voices of the people who lived in the neighborhood and giving back. They started rebuilding homes and offering houses at minimal costs to some of the Trenton residents. They even donated homes to the volunteers who worked day in and day out to gut these houses. The volunteers would put in 200 hours and then their name would go on a list to receive a rebuilt house. They would only be responsible for the taxes on the house. The after school program, Boy Scouts and the summer program was added to this agenda to give kids in the neighborhood an opportunity to get off the streets.

After a few short months, we all became a part of this center. Every day after school we all would head down to the Martin House instead of going home. It was fun and most of my friends were down there. Every Friday we would either go swimming or play basketball at a local gym. My older brothers even became camp counselors. It didn't pay much but it did give them a sense of responsibility. If they were late to work or didn't show up Father Bill would dock their pay.

Almost Home

For the next four years I was a constant member of the Martin House program as a student. Even after moving out of the Wilbur Section, I would still make the trip over there after school. My mother even started to volunteer at the center and help the kids. She also became involved in the housing programs. With all of the hours she put in, my mother became eligible to receive a house. After moving from my grandmother's house, we moved into a two-bedroom apartment in the Mill Hill Section of Trenton. It was nice but very small. We were all excited because it appeared that we would be able to move into a bigger house and we would finally get our own rooms. My mother was on the waiting list for about six months and one day she got the call from the Martin House.

Because my mother was an active member in the Martin House, everyone down at the Center wanted to make sure she got a very nice house. A four bedroom and two bathroom house was built for my mother on Clinton Ave in Trenton. This was by far the biggest house they ever built. We went to look at the house. It was very big and it was nice as hell. It had three floors, a huge basement and a back yard. Everything was brand new. The kitchen looked like something I had seen before on television. Although my mother loved the house, there was one major problem. My mother had to turn down the house because she didn't like the neighborhood. The house was located near the corner of Clinton Ave and Olden Ave. To this day, this is one of the worst neighborhoods in all of Trenton. It hurt my mother to turn down the house because it would have been the first house that she could have actually called her own. There was enough room for all of us and then some. It was three times as big as the apartment that we were living in over in Mill Hill. But my mother did not want to put us in harms way. She decided not to take the house. My mother went back on the waiting list, but her number never came up again.

The Boy Scouts

When I turned 13, I joined the Boys Scouts. Our troop was Troop #257. We had a meeting every Wednesday, wore a uniform and had to pay fifty cents a week for dues. Every meeting we had to recite the Boy Scout oath and also tell of a good deed that we did during the week. If you didn't have a good deed, couldn't pay your dues or was unable to recite the Boy Scout oath, you had to do 50-100 push-ups. The Boy Scouts gave me a sense of belonging and I was proud that I belonged to something big. The full uniform was $50.00 by the time you got everything that belonged on it. It was a cool organization of which to be apart. I felt proud.

Father Brian was the Scout Master. Every year he assigned a Troop Leader to watch over the other troops and made sure they were doing things correctly. We had a handbook that we had to read and the goal for every scout was to become an Eagle Scout. There were many steps in between which required much time and dedication but everybody had their eye on the Eagle Scout Badge.

Yards Creek

My first year in the Boy Scouts was very challenging. Trying to get badges and move up in rank was exciting and very difficult at the same time. Little did I know, this experience was about to get more challenging. During my first summer in the Boy Scouts, the troop leader gave us all permission slips for my mother to sign. It was for a Boy Scout retreat at Yards Creek. We were never away from the house for more than a day or so if it didn't involve family. This would be the first time we would leave the house for more than a few days. My mother quickly signed the permission slip and we were all set to go. There was a $50.00 fee to go My mother managed to get the money for us and we left a few weeks later.

When we first got there, it was about 200 yards of open field. There was a main office, a cafeteria and a general store. A little past all of that, there were the showers and the bathrooms. Once you pass that area, there was nothing else with electricity, water or any other conveniences that we were used to. Each troop master actually drove through the main entrance and into the woods. From what I remember, every year we were towards the back of the woods. Because we had a big troop, we would always get one of the bigger camp sites. There was also a lake, which was our swimming area. Canoes were there if we wanted to go on the lake, where we could learn how to fish. There were also different activities that we could do. I was excited about being away from the house and wanted to do every thing possible before I returned home.

There was one major problem with going to this camp every year. Troop 257 was an all black troop. All of the kids were predominantly from the Wilbur Section. We were all poor and all under privileged. Going to this camp was always a challenge because we were the only black troop up there out of 20 or so troops. It took some getting used to because we were constantly being blamed for a number of things and also singled out during disciplinary issues. It was almost as if we had to stick together and help each other out because we were not getting any support from the other troops, including the directors of the camp. But every year we went up there and tried to make our Scout Master proud. We made the best of it and tried to excel in all of the events.

The Raider

The Raider was a marathon-style race that was held every year. The race consisted of a one mile run, a canoe race for 2 miles and a hike for 3 miles. This was an endurance task. You would get a map of the entire facility. Throughout the woods you would have landmarks that would show you which way to go.

The second year I was there I decided to compete in the race. I'm not sure what possessed me to want to do it because I was nervous. This was only my second year at the camp and I wasn't conditioned to do such a race. I trained for it the day before the races as I tried to build some type of endurance through running and other exercises. I had already run cross-country track for a year in high school so I thought I would be good and could compete with the other participants. My troop encouraged me a lot and wished me luck.

As I walked to the starting block and got ready to go, I could feel everybody looking at me. From the looks on their faces, they didn't believe that I could do this race much less finish it altogether. And the truth was all I wanted to do was finish. Whether I won or not didn't really matter to me. A lot of those faces were white and they wanted me to fail. It was written all over their faces. I remember starting the race and reminding myself not to start off fast. The first three hundred yards was all up hill. I had to run up over the mountain to the other side to get to the lake and hop in the canoe. There were about ten or eleven of us competing in the race. I started in fourth place and kept the pace. All I could think about was that I didn't have the right shoes and that I was tired already. This was something totally different than the cross-country track. I got up hill and found myself in last place. I never ran up hill before and wasn't ready for that task. I was about to stop as I approached the top of the mountain but I hated losing so I didn't give up. I couldn't look like a loser to all of these people.

When I stopped, I lost a lot of steam and I had to get it back quickly. The key to winning these kinds of races was to get a pace and keep it no matter who was running faster or slower than you were. I began walking up the hill to regain my pace and figured by that time I was going to come in last place. I alternated between walking and climbing until I was able to have enough stamina to run again. It was beneficial for me to stop because I was able to catch my breath. I got to the top and looked over. All of the other boy scouts were flying down the hill, some out of control because the mountain was steep.

That's when a major fear came over me. I've always been afraid of heights. When I looked over and really saw how steep it was I wanted to quit. What I found myself doing was walking down. Again, all I wanted to do was to finish. I walked faster and faster until I was running. Not too fast but I had a good rhythm. When I got to the bottom of the hill, I noticed that there were eight people in front of me. Apparently a few of the other troops fell down the hill.

So I was no longer in last place trying to get to the lake. I approached a one-person canoe. I threw on the life jacket even though I knew how to swim. I just wanted to finish. I got in the canoe and started to row. As I'm rowing, I tried to breathe how I was taught while running cross-country because I was getting cramps in my stomach. The people who were in front of me were struggling just like I was and maybe two or three people had a good lead on me. I was thinking in the back of my mind that I should quit. I was only in the middle of the lake and had a long way to go. I was tired and discouraged. Finally I got around the bank and saw the finish line. I saw the dock where I would be pulling in at and a huge sign that read FINISH LINE. By then I'm in fifth place. I was making fairly good time because I refused to quit despite how winded I was. When I got to the side, I had to throw these heavy boots on as well as a backpack. In the backpack was a flashlight, a canteen, some trail mix and other little things to get me through the rest of the race. It felt like a ton of bricks. My legs began to hurt from the run, my stomach was touching my spine and my arms by then were numb. The people on the sidelines gave me a map. The red part was a straight shot through and the yellow part was a short cut but had fewer clues than the red part. If you deviated from the two given paths, you automatically lost and were disqualified.

As I walked I looked for the red dots to ensure I was going the right way. As long as the sun was out I had a chance. But if I couldn't find my way in the woods and the sun went down, I was going to be in big trouble. There were snakes out there, raccoons, all types of bugs and I heard of a few bear sightings too. If you're prepared, which I was, you could manage but it was tough. I began to walk fast at times. My eyes were wide as hell because I was looking for everything. The other two guys in front of me were gone. I couldn't see them at all. I tried to keep my focus and concentrate on finishing. Step by step I began to pick up the pace. All of a sudden I see this red and orange snake and it looked like a tree branch. Up at Yards Creek, there were two snakes that were the most popular. There was the Black Racer and the Copper Head snake. The Copper Head snake was poisonous. The Black Racer wasn't poisonous but it was fast. This snake was a Copper Head. I stepped right over it and hit a twig. I thought I stepped on the snake but what I heard was a snap. The Copper Head went right after the branch. I was so freaked out. Just as I heard it I ran my ass off. The backpack and boots were no longer a hindrance. I didn't blow my whistle or anything I just ran about 600 yards. When I cleared the brushes, I found myself to be in like third place.

Once I got out of the woods I saw an opening. It was an open field that I had to walk across and enter more woods. That's where the other two guys were. I heard the others behind me and I knew that I was making good time. I ran across the field and walked through the second set of woods. I wanted badly to blow my whistle and just quit but I couldn't. My heart wouldn't let me. These woods were more rugged. There were a lot of sliding rocks and small creeks. When I got down towards the end, I saw one guy in front of me this time. I thought that I was about to win. I dropped my bag off and ran the last few yards to the finish line. I made a mad dash and the guy in front of me was running his ass off. I was so winded as I approached and crossed the finish line.

As it turned out I ended up in fifth place. The other three guys were so far ahead that I couldn't see them. When I found out that I came in fifth place I was disappointed. I felt like a failure. For a minute I couldn't get it together. Everybody else was so happy because I was the only one from our troop that completed the race. I never realized that no one ever tried it before me. So I became the first member of Troop #257 to finish the Raider. And that was a better feeling than winning the race.

The Olympics

Another event that was very big at Yards Creek was the Boy Scout Olympics. Every year they would hold these series of games for the different troops to compete in. Having been the only black troop at Yards Creek, we were looked down upon and to a certain extent we played into the stereotype. We acted overly tough and didn't show up to certain events. Basically we were rebels and we never took the Olympics serious.

I remember my last year there, Father Brian came to us and he wanted to know if we were serious about any of the Olympics. He tried to explain the importance of participating and sometimes even winning. He was disappointed that we didn't take them seriously. We only would do the Olympics if we felt like it. It was no big deal to us. My older brother Mike stepped up and said that he *did* want to try to win it. I looked at Mike and could see that he was serious. He wanted to go to Yards Creek and win the Olympics. That particular year we were determined with Mike's encouragement to make sure we had the fastest runner competing for the track portion, the fastest swimmer swimming for us and so on. When we got to the actual Olympics we were focused. But getting and keeping this mindset was no easy task. We had a huge fight with another troop from Jersey.

Earlier that week our tents were raided. Some things were stolen from our tents including my brother's watch. When we were all at the lake he'd seen one of the other troop members with his watch on. So he went and got some of his boys and they got into a huge fight. It was so bad that we almost got sent home. But after everything had calmed down, both troops were forced to shake hands and become friends again. Despite the altercation with the other troop we were still determined to win and put our best foot forward. We got to the Olympic site about a half an hour early. The earlier fight had everyone pumped and we ended up taking 5 of the 8 possible events. There were a few events that were contested and we ended up winning 3 events. There was another team that had also won 3 events. As fate would have it, the troop that won the three events was the same troop we were fighting with earlier.

For the tiebreaker, we had to pick an event out of a hat. We ended up picking archery, an event that we lost in an earlier contest. None of our troop members were good at shooting a bow and arrow so Mike stepped up to represent the troop. He and one of the scouts from the enemy troop went to compete for the gold. We had to stay behind. Because no one was good in this event we figured we would come in second place and lose the competition.

It took about twenty minutes and they were back. Mike came in the mess hall and was jumping up and down. We all looked at each other and began jumping up and down with him. He'd won and we were taking the Olympics award home with us while beating the other team who'd raided out tents. Winning the events gave us tremendous confidence in ourselves and proved that teamwork could prevail. By beating the odds and overcoming the obstacles Troop #257 had quite a few reasons to be proud.

4
Joanne Smith

My mother was pregnant with her first child at the age of 15. Within six short years, she gave birth to four children, all boys. Although she tried her best not to show it, I know it was very rough on her trying to raise us right and keep her head above water at the same time. And despite all of the problems she had and the rough times we encountered, she was always supportive of us in everything we set out to do or desired to accomplish. If I had to use one word to describe my mother it would be *supportive*. She always wanted to see us do good and hoped that we would make the right decisions in life. My mother did many things for me. She's one of the main reasons why I strive to be the best and why my work ethic is ridiculous. I watched my mother work hard my entire life and cannot remember a time when my mother was unemployed or just stayed home and didn't work. She always worked because she had to take care of four boys. My mother could've easily been a bad person. She could've chose to party all night long, go out drinking and smoking but she never showed us that. My ability to go hard over a long period of time and stay on the grind comes from her. I watched her do it for so many years. She held it down for us.

The thing about my mother that always impressed me was that no matter what we wanted to do, whether it had to do with school, with rap groups or even girls, she was there for us 100%. If we wanted or needed anything she would do her best to make it happen. I could've grown up to be a garbage man and she would've supported me. That sticks out when I think about my mother. She taught me serious life lessons without having to sit me down and lecture me.

Integrity

When I was about nine years old my mother taught me a serious lesson on integrity. I was still living at 14 Hampton Avenue. One day my father came by to pick us up to visit my paternal grandmother. She didn't live very far but it was always nice to visit her. On this particular day we were there hanging out with my older cousin Mark. All of my brothers admired Mark because he ran track. He was a fast sprinter and he even competed on the highest level. He used to workout a lot and we used to imitate him and try to workout with him. To stay in shape, he would run around the track at the high school.

As soon as we got to my grandmother's house I kept asking him if I could go jogging with him. He told me to ask my father. I ran in the house and tried to ask my father if I could go, but he was busy. By the time I ran back downstairs Mark was gone. He'd left me. I ran to the back porch but he wasn't there. Because my father was busy and my grandmother wasn't around, I just decided to leave without telling anyone. I was running down the street when I saw my cousin turn the corner. I picked up the pace to try and catch him so I could jog side by side with him. When I turned the corner he was already down the next street and turning the corner. I started to sprint really fast and went to cross the street. Then everything went black.

When I woke up, I was laying on the side of the street. This guy was standing above me when I opened my eyes. He kept asking my name but I couldn't open my mouth. I passed out again. The next time I woke up I was in an ambulance. They had the oxygen mask on my face to maintain my breathing level. I could see but couldn't focus and I didn't see anybody I knew. I passed out again. When I woke up this time I was in the hospital. I was lying on my side because my back was badly bruised. I was leaning over and all I saw was my mother's face. She was holding my hand while she cried. I looked over at her and could see that she was hurting. I'd never seen her like that before.

While I was running across the street, a pick-up truck hit me. It was a truck registered to a floral company. According to the police report, the truck was going about 35-45 miles per hour. The driver didn't have time to stop when he saw me and ended up hitting me flat on my back because of the way I was running. I was running diagonally across the street and I didn't even see him. I got hit, flew up in the air and hit the sidewalk. Apparently, I jumped up and ran to a neighbor's house. I started banging on the door and a guy came to the door. I told him that somebody got hit and then I passed out. The guy knew our family and went to my grandmother's house to get my mother and father.

I had two broken ribs from being hit and was messed up for a long time. When I woke up all I could think about was my mother being mad at me because I left without her permission. My mother told me to be quiet and rest. My entire back was swollen and bloody. I don't remember crying. The doctor took x-rays to see how bad I was off. I couldn't go to school for about a week.

My mother had every right to be mad at me. But instead of being upset, my parents and extended family focused more on making sure that I was okay. For the next week or two my father was around a lot and made sure that I was all right. That was a good feeling because they were separated and he wasn't living with us at the time. All of the family came around my grandmother's house to look after me. I stayed over my father's mother's house for a few days then left and went back over to my paternal grandmother's house. For weeks, I had to sleep on my side instead of my back. I also had to go through some rehabilitation. The guy who informed my grandmother of my accident came over to the house and the guy who hit me sent me cards and flowers. My father wanted to sue him but my mother didn't. I'd found out later that the guy was speeding. To this day, I have back problems and back pain. I still played sports and remained physically active but haven't been the same since. The one scar that I take away from that was the look on my mothers face and how hurt she was. I'm pretty sure she knew I wasn't going to die but learning that a truck had hit me probably had her going crazy. The look on her face will forever be burned in my mind and I never want her to go through that again. Another observation that affects me to this day is the fact that my mother didn't seek legal action against the company. She didn't sue the guy even though she knew that she could've gotten a lot of money and our lives could've changed for the better. She just didn't think that it was right and didn't want to add insult to injury. I never questioned it but as I got older I knew we could've used the extra money. My mother always played it straight and showed us how to be the bigger person. I was alive and to her that was priceless. It showed my mother's integrity and the type of woman she was and still is.

Support

Once we moved from the Wilbur Section over to the Mill Hill section of Trenton, I transferred to another school. I was in fifth grade at the time. Moving from one elementary school to the next was interesting. I was growing up fast and making a lot of friends. Once I started this new school in south Trenton, it would be no different. I met a lot of people, had a lot of friends and got in the mix really quick. I found out quickly who the cool kids were, where to hang out at after school and who not to mess

45

with.   After about two weeks at the new school I noticed that all the kids dressed alike. Because my father used to dress us up all the time, to "dress hip-hop" was new to me.   I looked like a geek to everybody else. I definitely stood out.

One day when I got home, I rummaged through my brother's clothes to try to improve my wardrobe.   I asked to borrow his jeans.   He understood and was cool with it.   I wore them to school and was feeling comfortable.   But I was missing one thing that everybody else had; a hat. Everybody in south Trenton was wearing Kangols at the time.   I was like damn; I got to get one of those hats.   There were a few stores in my neighborhood that had them so I went looking for them.   They cost five dollars at the time.   I didn't have the money so I asked my older brother for the money.   He didn't have it so I had to ask my mother.   My mother had the money but she didn't know where to buy the hat. She didn't want to just give me the money, she wanted to pick it up herself.   I remember when LL Cool J was wearing the hat in a video.   When the video came on I showed her and she finally got the hat for me.   I wore it to school and I was happy.   I was good then. The hat was all I needed.

The day I wore the hat to school I began to get a response that was much unexpected. Instead of complimenting me on my hat a few kids were laughing at me.   You can tell when somebody is laughing at you and trying not to let you see them.   A few kids clicked up and were pointing at my hat and pointing at me.   They were laughing really hard. Even those who I called my friends were laughing.   I couldn't ask anybody because then I'd really look like a fool. After school I went to the YMCA wearing my hat. Here I am again thinking I'm cool but I'm getting the same response. People were still laughing at me. But instead of finding out what was so funny I just tried my best to look cool. People were laughing so hard that they were crying and rolling on the floor. I don't know why I didn't ask to find out what the joke was all about. I just left it alone and went home.

When I got home I tried to find out what the hell was so funny. Did I have something in my teeth? Did I have a ketchup stain on my shirt? Did I have mixed matched socks on? What was it? I took my hat off and put it down and I finally realized why they were laughing. For anyone that knows, the Kangol is spelled "KANGOL" and it has a kangaroo on it. That was the cool thing about it. I looked at my hat and the logo was spelled KENGGO and pictured a dinosaur instead of a kangaroo. I was so angry that I threw it in the trash. I was mad at my mother for not getting the right one because people had a field day on me. They were laughing like they were crazy and then of course I made it worse because I kept thinking about it. I'd just started at this school and I felt as though everybody thought I was a clown.

A couple of months later my mother had asked me about the hat. I lied and told her that I lost it. Looking back, I know my mother was just looking out for me. She didn't do it on purpose; she just didn't know. It was a bootleg KANGOL. Everybody was taking advantage of the bootleg thing. I feel bad about how I reacted. I just wanted to be cool, and my mother did what she could to help me. I lost sight of that while worrying about what other people, I didn't even know, were saying. Her intentions were to make me happy.

Street Smarts

By 16, I was working two jobs, running a rap group, trying to make it to college and was involved in every school activity possible. I was in the choir, on and off the track team and acting in the school plays. In the middle of my junior year I learned one of the biggest lessons of my life.

My brother Steven was always involved with plays and performing. I saw a few plays that he performed in and wanted to do the same thing he was doing. So when I saw a posting to be an actor in one of the school plays I decided to try out for the part. I got the part and performed in the play a few months later. The play ran for about two weeks and I did a great job.

I had a very close friend that performed in the play with me. His name was Kevin. A few of the nights he decided to bring his family to the performances to support us. Before one of the performances, Kevin introduced me to his mother and his older cousin Tanya. She said she was happy to meet me and wished me luck on the performance. I didn't think anything of her at the time. I just said hello and stayed focused on the performance. When the play was over Kevin's cousin approached me again and told me that I did a great job. The next day in school Kevin was upset with me. He kept asking me why I blew his cousin off. I didn't think I was being mean to her. I was having problems at home at the time so I was really oblivious to her liking me and didn't pay it too much attention.

The next night was the last day of the performance and Kevin decided to bring his entire family, including Tanya. I told him that I was going to make a better effort to pay attention to his cousin. After the performance was over we all made a long curtain call and signed autographs for our new fans. Just like every other performance she attended, Tanya walked up to me and told me that I did a great job. I paid special attention to her this time. She was about 5'8, long hair, very cute face and very friendly. There was something in her face that immediately attracted me to her. It was her age. Tanya was clearly older than me. I could tell by the way she spoke to me. I think that is why I didn't pay attention to her before. Tanya told me that she was attracted to me from the first time she saw the play and told Kevin to introduce us. She asked me how old I was. When I told her that I was sixteen she looked surprised and then she laughed.

"You're only sixteen?"

"Yup, why? Do I look younger?"

"No you look older. I thought you were graduating this year."

"Nah, not for another year. Why? How old are you?"

"I'm twenty. I'll be twenty one in a few months".

When she told me that she was twenty my jaw dropped. I was like damn she is really rocking the cradle. But she was too cute for me to walk away from her. She gave me her number and told me to call her. I was nervous but took it anyway. I called her a few days later and we started kicking it. She came up to the school one day and she took me to the movies. She had a car for the first few months that we were dating but lost it in a car accident. I told my friends about her and how old she was and everybody thought I was lying. I started telling her to meet me outside after school just so I could show her off to my friends. Shortly there after, she asked me why I didn't invite her over to my house. I knew that my mother would have a problem with it but I let her come over anyway.

The first time she came over I introduced her to my mother as one of my friends. The first question that my mother asked was what school she went to. She quickly lied to my mother and told her that she graduated the year before. On top of that, she told her that she was eighteen and about to turn nineteen. My mother let me have her over as company but we had to stay in the living room. When Tanya left, my mother asked me where I'd met her. She didn't trip but she was cautious. I saw Tanya a little bit later and questioned her on why she lied to my mom about her age. She thought that my mother would be mad and wouldn't let us date each other. To me it wasn't a big deal. I didn't see us as boyfriend and girlfriend. We were just friends at the time.

After she lied to my mother, I didn't let her come to my house again. I always went to her house. Her mother was never home. It was always just her and her sister. One day I called her and told her that I wanted to see her. She told me that it wasn't a good time because she was busy. When I hung up the phone she called me back about two minutes later. She told me that it was okay if I came over. She wanted me to give her an hour or so. To kill time I went over my friend Mike's house. He stayed around the corner from her so it all worked out. He knew about Tanya and it turned out that we had more in common. He too was seeing an older woman. He asked me if we had sex or not and I told him that we didn't. We kissed and did some preliminary stuff but I was a little too nervous to go all the way. After an hour, I asked Mike to come with me over to Tanya's house. He agreed and we left.

We got to Tanya's house and I knocked on the door. Somebody on the other side of the door answered. There was only one problem. It was a dude's voice.

"Who is it?"

"It's Dashawn"

"Who are you looking for?"

"Tanya"

Nothing. I looked in the window then knocked on the door and still no response. I went to a pay phone and called her but got no answer. I went back to the house and knocked again and again no one answered. I was confused because I'd just spoken to her an hour ago. I asked Mike if he heard a voice and he said yes. So we just left and I went home.

As soon as I got back home my phone was ringing off the hook. It was Tanya.

"Why didn't you stop by to see me?"

"I did stop by and some nigga answered the door but never opened it!"

"What are you talking about? I was waiting for you and you never showed up."

"Ok, you know what? I'm not going to argue with you. We are not together and it's no big deal. Some dude asked who I was and who I was there to see. I answered and I didn't hear nothing else."

"You are trippin'. My doorbell never rung."

"Goodbye, I'm hanging up."

I hung up the phone and decided not to call her again. We were just friends at the time and I didn't want to deal with the stress. About a month later she called me and wanted to take me out. I agreed and the rollercoaster ride got even worse.

This time she decided to drive over to my house. Instead of going out she wanted to stay there and talk. My mother was nowhere to be found so I let her stay. We talked for a couple of hours and she told me how much she missed me and how she was happy to see me. Although I was hesitant to admit it, I missed her too. After a few hours of talking she wanted to go to my room. Something told me not to do it but I was sixteen and very curious about this older woman so I took her down to my bedroom in the basement. When she got to my room our conversations became very sexual.

"So why you never tried to have sex with me? Because I'm older than you?"

"Nah. To be honest I was just a little intimidated by you."

"Are you serious?"

"Yes I am."

She told me that there was no reason to be intimidated by her. She told me that she wanted me from the first time she met me. Hearing that from her really turned me on. In fact, most things about her turned me on, I was just too nervous to tell her. A few minutes later we began to kiss and she was getting really aggressive. She was talking shit and that was turning me on. She kept asking me if I was attracted to her and if I wanted her. I kept saying yes until she got naked. She just took off her clothes, no questions asked and all I kept thinking about is what would happen if my mother came home. I would be in trouble. On the other hand I was like "damn"! I wasn't going to front and act like I knew what I was doing. I was definitely too young to be a playboy. I wasn't a virgin at that time but I was definitely too inexperienced for her. So I just let her lead the way. We were doing some heavy kissing by now and I knew it was about to go down. I tried to get up and get a condom but she grabbed me.

"What are you doing?"

"Getting a condom."

"What do you need that for? You don't trust me?"

It wasn't that I didn't trust her. The last thing I needed at the time was a baby. I'd only had sex a few times before that and I always used condoms. All I could remember was my father telling me to always protect myself and to not be a fool. I told her that I trusted her and she told me that she wasn't having sex with anybody else. As much as she was trying to convince me, I just couldn't bring myself to have unprotected sex. I ended up getting one and putting it on. We had sex and it was good. I wasn't a pro but she wasn't disappointed. In fact, after that day in the basement we started seeing each other seriously. We were boyfriend and girlfriend officially.

A few months went by and we were going strong. We would go out on a few dates and I would sneak over to her house on occasions and we would have sex. I always made it a point to use condoms. I was too afraid of the consequences of not wearing one. There would be days when I would call her and couldn't find her. I would ask where she'd been and she could not give me a straight answer. I didn't want to appear too possessive so I would drop the subject. She was older than I was so I figured she just had a different life than I had. One night she called me around 11 o'clock. I was expecting her to tell me that she was missing me or she wanted to see what I was doing the next day. But this time she had some different news for me.

"Hey this is Tanya."

"I know who this is. How are you doing?"

"Not so good. I got some bad news the other day."

"Really? What's going on? Everything ok?"

"Nope. I'm pregnant Dashawn."

I just got quiet. I really could not believe it. It felt like I was in a movie and the camera zoomed in on my face really quick. All I could see is the look on my mother's face. Shit. Tanya wasn't sad or happy. She just nonchalantly told me that she was pregnant and that she needed to do something. I asked her if she was sure and she said yes. She'd already been to the doctor.

I was scared! I was about to be a father. I called Mike Green and told him that I needed to talk to him. I walked over to his house around one o'clock in the morning and told him what happened. Mike lived with his girlfriend and already had a kid. I asked him what he thought and he told me that I needed to find out if she was going to keep it or not. Then after talking for a while he came out and asked me if the baby was even mine. Prior to his asking I hadn't even thought about the possibility of the baby not being mine. I believed it was mine because she said it was and I wasn't thinking that she was trying to set me up. All I knew was that I used a condom and maybe it was punctured or it slipped off. I didn't know what to think, but when he said that, I sat there and began to question if she would play me out like that. Mike was always more advanced and more on point than I was when it came to life. He had dropped out of school, had a child and was living with his girlfriend; so he was definitely more seasoned on the issues of being in relationships and dealing with girls.

When I was walking back home, I was so scared. I wasn't crying or anything but I was just shocked. I got home about four in the morning and I had called her up. I told her that I would be by tomorrow after work to talk to her. She wanted to talk but I really wasn't in the mood. I needed to think. She told me that there wasn't anything to think about because there was no way that she could have the baby. Again I was shocked. I didn't understand why and it never crossed my mind that she had no intentions on keeping the baby. We agreed to talk the next day.

The following day I went to see her. She told me she was four months pregnant. I had to think back to what Mike's girlfriend looked like at four months pregnant. With the memory fresh in my mind and looking at Tanya, she didn't look pregnant to me. In the middle of our talk she told me that she told her mother about it. Her mother wasn't upset with me. She had recommended a doctor that we could go see for an abortion, which would cost $400. First of all, I didn't have $400 for an abortion and secondly, I wondered if I had any say in the matter. One day she tells me she's pregnant and the next day she tells me that she wants $400 for an abortion. At that point I told her that I needed to tell my mother. Tanya questioned me and wanted to know about the money but I had made up my mind how I was going to handle it.

I got home and none of my brothers were around for me to talk to. I waited for my mother to get home. Waiting for my mother to get home felt like an eternity. I was sweating from pondering on different mental scenarios of how I was going to tell her the news. I knew she was going to be disappointed and I remembered the look on her face when I was in the hospital from being hit by that truck. I never wanted to see her like that again.

My mother came home and I told her that I needed to talk to her. I started rambling and she just looked at me like I was crazy. She asked me what happened and I told her the whole story. I thought she was going to flip out but the first thing she asked was who Tanya was. Since I never brought her around like that, my mother wasn't familiar with her and our relationship, which was six months long at that point. She remembered me bringing an older girl to meet her, but since she didn't see her come by the house after that, my mother pretty much forgot about her. She was silent for a split second. Then my mother came out and said that it wasn't mine. I asked her how she knew that. I had just admitted to sleeping with her and although we used a condom, I was aware that accidents do happen. She shook her head to say "no" and insisted that it wasn't mine. My mother told me that the next time Tanya called she wanted to speak to her. Feeling confused I had to agree to that.

Tanya called a few hours later and I told her that I spoke to my mother. I also told her that my mother didn't think that the baby was mine and she wanted to talk to her. Before I could get out a word my mother picked up the phone and began to speak to Tanya.

"Hello is this Tanya?"

"Yes"

"The same Tanya who lied to me about her age?"

"Yes but I didn't lie to — "

"Oh ok. Listen, I know that you think you're pregnant by Dashawn, but you're not. He said he used protection with you and I believe him. But good luck finding the real father."

That's all my mother said and she hung up the phone. She didn't scream or yell. That really surprised me because I thought we were in for a big argument on the phone. *Now* I had to play chess with Tanya and basically be the bad guy. I told her that until we find out if the baby is mine I wasn't going to do anything. I hung up the phone while she was in mid sentence and an hour later the phone rang again. It was Tanya's mother and she asked for me. I got on the phone and she went off on me. She reiterated that it was my kid and I told her what my mother said. So she wanted to speak to somebody by the name of Diane. Well since my mothers name isn't Diane, I had no idea who she was talking about. Then Tanya picked up the phone and asked her mother to hang up. I was baffled. I was confused and had no idea what was going on. I hung up the phone. Tanya called me back and wanted to come to talk to me.

When she got there she apologized for getting pregnant. My mother was home at that time. She came downstairs while we were talking and told Tanya that she better not be trying to game me and that she needed to find her baby's daddy because I wasn't it. Tanya began to cry because my mother was screaming and was adamant in her beliefs. And even though my mother didn't know the whole story, she was sure this wasn't my baby. Tanya was an emotional wreck and I felt bad for her. I didn't know why she was crying. At that moment Tanya decided to be honest and admitted to having sex with another dude without a condom. She said she automatically assumed it was mine. I guess when my mother didn't budge; Tanya felt she had no other choice but to tell us.

I walked her home and when we got there, some dude was waiting there for her. He asked her where she'd been. This was too crazy for me. I looked at her and I knew he was the dude she told me about. He wasn't really paying attention to me so I left before anything jumped off. Two days later she called me and told me that she really liked me. The dude who was there was her ex-boyfriend and she came clean with a lot of stuff. I just listened to her story without responding. If I didn't walk her home and witness her lies for myself I don't know how long I would have believed in her and her lies.

For my mother to have the foresight to see that this was a game from the door was amazing to me. I never questioned my mother. I always believed that she was the only one really down for me. My mother knew exactly what was going on before she knew the details. I remember my mother telling me "if someone would lie to your mother, they would definitely lie to you." I never forgot that statement.

As far as Tanya, she never had the child. I haven't seen her since. I assumed her ex-boyfriend paid for her to have an abortion. After he heard the news about Tanya and me, her cousin Kevin and I stopped being friends. I didn't feel it necessary to disclose all the details about what went down. Enough damage was done to the both of us.

5

Michael Taylor, Sr.

Throughout my childhood I was always questioned about my audacity to aspire to be successful. Outside of my family and closest friends I was not encouraged by many to do better. In fact, most of my plans and dreams were met with constant doubt and disbelief. Those who wanted to see me fail could not understand why a person in my situation even believed that I had a shot. I have to credit my father with lighting a fire under my ass to be successful. For as long as I could remember my father would never miss an opportunity to school us and tell us that we could do anything we put our minds to. My father would keep us up late at night talking to us about staying out of trouble and staying on the right path. But my father did more than just *talk* to keep us focused.

My father was from the old school. He believed in discipline. As a teenager, he ran the streets and got into a lot of trouble. He would always say that his worse nightmare was to watch us follow his footsteps and make the same mistakes. To make sure we didn't slip up he refused to spare the rod. I never got a beating from my mother. But my father definitely made up for that. To put it in perspective, my father was in and out of my life while I was living in Trenton. But when he was there he kept us all in check with ease. My cousins would joke with us all the time about how we would act up when my father wasn't around. And then he would come by and we would all act like angels. When he was around we were in line and when he was gone, we were a little out of control, and it was this balance that shaped the person that I am today. Growing up I got into trouble. And then on the flip side, I stayed focused enough to make things happen. There were a number of situations that happened when my father was present that helped me stay on the right path.

Stick Around

My father's mother lived in Willingboro, New Jersey. She had a very nice house. Going to my grandmother's house was like going on a vacation to us. The neighborhood was safer, her house was cleaner and she always had food. She lived alone and was separated from my grandfather for a very long time. My grandmother was independent. When she was younger, she owned a beauty salon, three houses and was always about making money. When we were at her house, it was always about letting go and just relaxing. We left our worries and troubles back at home. At that time we were living in the Mill Hill section of Trenton.

My grandmother did, however, have a back door that didn't lock. She would place a stick on the slide track and that would stop anyone from sliding the door open. One day, I don't know why, I decided to take the stick. I took the stick, hopped on my bike and headed to a park that was in the neighborhood. With the stick in hand I banged it against everything I saw. The stick eventually broke and I just left it there. When I got back to the house, I was playing in the back yard. No one asked me where I went. My father decided that we were going to see my aunt and uncles and told us to meet him at the car. When my grandmother went to close the back door she noticed that the stick was gone. And although she lived in a nice area and there was no chance someone would even attempt to come to her back door, she was very upset that she couldn't find it. My father eventually got upset and asked us where the stick was. Now it clicked. I took the stick and I broke it down at the park.

I wasn't really saying anything at first but we also weren't leaving until the stick was found. So I eventually told him that I'd taken the stick and that I'd lost it. He got upset immediately. My father had, and still has a way of looking at you, which would let you know that he was mad. So instead of hitting me or giving me some type of punishment, my father told me that I had to stay there and couldn't go with them. I was only eleven and he said that I had to watch the door and make sure no one came in. Everyone left and I was in tears. I was scared because all I can remember was that he had said to watch the door and

I kept thinking that at any given moment, someone was going to come through the door.

So I grabbed a knife, walked around the house while still crying trying to see if anyone was in the house. About a half an hour later, the biggest thunderstorm came. It was like a scene in a scary movie. Anything that made a sound had my body trembling. I couldn't believe that I was stuck there. The thunder was extra loud. I went and sat in the kitchen. Through the kitchen you could see the garage and I was hoping to see my father pull up. The television and light was on. A huge crackle of thunder pounded and the electricity went out. I remained seated in the kitchen and cried. After a while, the rain subsided and I stopped crying. An hour later, they came home. The lights came back on, the rain had stopped. I wasn't scared anymore, I was angry. I was so mad at my father for making me stay there by myself. I was wishing that a gang of stuff, a bus, a plane or whatever hit him so that he would know how angry I was at him. Looking back, I know my father wanted to teach me a lesson and to a certain extent, he wanted to toughen me up. I'm sure he knew that no one would break into the house and that I'd be safe.

Boys Will Be Boys

A few years later I joined the Boy Scouts and headed up to Yards Creek for the summer retreat. It was around the time that our tents were raided by another Boy Scout troop. We later found out that the other troop stole a lot of stuff from the tents and we were very upset. Being the only black troop at the camp did not help the situation. It was definitely a lot of racial tension brewing around the camp. Certainly, we had a few bad apples in the troop but the majority of the kids were well behaved. When we had the problem with the other troop, it lasted for two days. I clearly remember that during the week, although we all fought together, there were a few individual fights as well. The one thing that went on with me during that time happened when we were all at the lake. My brothers Mike and Steven, two other troop members and I were walking back to the campsite. On the way back we ran into two of the younger boys from the other troop. We stopped them. I really didn't know what we were going to do. One of Mike's friends asked them why they took his watch. They tried to act like they didn't know much about the situation. Because Mike and his friend were too big to do anything, they looked at me and told me to hit them. I didn't want to. They clearly were scared and didn't want to fight. But my brother's friend said that if I didn't hit one of them, he would hit me. So I hit the dude and at first he just looked at me. I could tell that he didn't want to fight. My older brother told me to hit him again. So I hit him again. He still didn't do anything. So Mike said, "okay, it's over let's roll" but my brother's friend, insisted that I hit him again. I hit him for the third time and he started crying. Clearly he didn't want to have any problems and we weren't even sure that these two boys had anything to do with our tents being raided.

It was over and we walked away. When I got home from the trip, my father was there and wanted to know what had happened at the camp. Apparently, the troop master contacted the parents of the children who were involved in the fight at the camp and my mother had called my father. We told him what happened. Mike was sixteen at the time and he was laughing about it with my father. Then Steven told my father about the fight that I had. They explained it to my father in a way that revealed that I didn't *want* to fight. My father asked for an explanation and my brothers continued to explain it in more detail, and included the fact that the boys were white. My father's mood immediately changed. At first he seemed to not be troubled about the situation and how it was handled, but when he found out that the boys were white, it was clear that he was uneasy with the situation. He was scared for me and upset with me. I told him that my brothers and his friend made me do it. It was either hit or be hit. My father ended up beating me for that. I didn't understand why he did that for a long time.

A few years later I thought about the situation. I figured that he was fearful of what may happen to me for beating on a white boy and also wanted to teach me that I shouldn't get caught up in that type of mess. Again, I was always looked at as the one that was going to do great things and this type of behavior could only hinder my growth. He didn't want me to begin a cycle of fighting and making wrong decisions based on what other people say or think. I didn't want to fight the boy and the boy clearly didn't want any issues with me. Yet thinking of what my brothers and their friend would do was far worse at the time than the circumstances that I could possibly face from beating on this kid. My father taught me that I needed to think for myself and think things through before I acted on anything.

Influence

For as long as I can remember I was always good with numbers. I was a quick learner from the door and my father noticed that in my early stages. He really wanted to nurture my strength with numbers and math and encouraged me to use them as much as I can. I began to see the results of my father's insistence when I was in the eight grade. I was in the gifted and talented program at Junior High #4. One of my math teachers, Mr. DeJesus nominated me for the National Achievement Award. This award was given to the best student in the school for any given subject that he or she over excelled in. I eventually won the award. I brought home the nomination to my mother and she was really excited. This award meant that my name would be listed in the United States Achievement Academy book. It served as a yearbook for all students nominated for this award. She shared this information with my father and he too was happy.

My father wasn't living with us at the time but was very active in our lives. He was a freelance photographer and he wanted to play an active part in helping me. The school needed a good picture of me to put in the book. My father came over and he brought me a suit and a tie. He worked at a photo lab and he took me there to take pictures of me. It was just he and I and that was special because it was very rare that just the two of us spent time together. We spent the whole day together. He took me to lunch and talked to me about college and what I could do if I graduated. He told me that he always knew that I would be the one to make great things happen. Even when I look at those pictures today, I can tell that I was proud of myself. And I believe that it was a result of my father's support and his belief in me. The expression on my face exerts pride and self-reverence. That was one of the last days we shared like that during my childhood.

After we took the pictures, he sent them in. He told everyone about my achievements, and went as far as to contact the local newspaper, the Trentonian. I received a letter from Doug Palmer, who was running for Mayor at the time, congratulating me on my achievements. My father framed it for me and I still have it today. In essence, my father instilled a lot of self-dignity in me and made me believe that I can do anything and make anything happen.

The Protector

My brother was dating this older girl when he was sixteen years old. She must've been about 12 years older than him. She would pick him up and take him places. At the time my father wasn't living with us and I knew my mother had a problem with the age difference. The girl was really cute, sexy and upfront with it and she reminded me of one of my mother's sisters. I remember my brother being so happy. She would spoil him, take him out to eat and buy him things. He didn't brag about her because he tried his best to keep their relationship under wraps. I don't know for sure if at the time they were having sex or not because we didn't talk like that.

One day my father came home. My brothers and I were home. The girl wasn't there at the time. He sat down and was talking to us when the girl came to the door and asked for my brother. My brother went to the door and invited her in thinking that he was going to show her off to my father and he'd be impressed. She came into the kitchen and my father just looked at her. My brother came back into the living room where we were and just sat down. I think he knew that my father wasn't too happy.

A few moments later my father called him into the kitchen and asked who the girl was. When my brother said that she was his girlfriend, my father looked everything but proud. He definitely didn't think that was a good thing. He looked over at the girl and she remained silent but confirmed my brother's statement with a simple nod. My father immediately went into attack mode with her.

"What the hell are you doing here?"

"What do you mean?"

"Do you know that my son is only 16?"

"Yes."

"And you don't see anything wrong with that?"

"No I don't."

He wasn't happy at all that this older woman was dating an under aged child. She was very nervous and didn't know what my father was going to do. He started to ask her more questions.

"Do you have a daughter?"

"Yes"

"And what if I told you that I wanted to date your daughter before she turned 18?"

"I would be upset!"

"Exactly. So get the hell out. And if I see you around my son again I'm going to call the police and have you arrested for statutory rape."

That was all he had to say. She was out the door. He told her that she had to go and my brother couldn't say anything. He didn't know what life she led or what type of person she was.

After that, I saw my father as our protector regardless of his absence in our everyday lives. It didn't matter that he didn't sleep at our house or that he didn't see us everyday. He was still our father and wanted nothing but the best for us. And I have to say that although he and my mother had their problems when it came to us, their sons, they always formed a united front in ensuring that we were taken care of mentally, physically and emotionally.

6
The Brothers

I can never imaging growing up without my brothers. And although we were all around the same age, we basically helped raise each other. Most of my personal traits, good and bad, can be traced back to my relationships with them in one way or another. I grew up with three brothers. I had three totally different relationships with each of them. And until my brother Mike left and went to college, we lived together all the time. Growing up with brothers was crazy at times. We all had different friends, different goals and different lives. We all had our individual problems and we each stayed with extra baggage. Sometimes we would get into trouble and instead of punishing one of us, my parents would punish us all. They figured that if someone else was there when the problem occurred, then we should have stopped it. Even though we had different personalities we managed to do a lot of things together. We were all in Boy Scouts together. We all went to summer camps and were in the choir together. At times we even went to the same school. Although we all had different personalities, it was hard to tell us apart because we looked so much alike. When my mother called out to us, she always called out all four of our names. It was amazing how we interacted as a whole. But individually each brother taught me many lessons about life.

Mike

Mike is the eldest child. Just like any other big brother, he was the leader. He tried things first, got all the girls and got into trouble first. As the oldest brother, he inspired the rest of us to do things that he was doing. Mike was a scout leader in the Boys Scouts so I wanted to be a scout leader. He ran track so I wanted to see if I could run track. He went to college and I made up my mind to go to college. He started to rap and than I started to rap. Even when my brother made mistakes or failed at something, I went behind him to try it to see if I could do it. I was always watching my brother to see how he reacted to situations and to see what type of decisions he made. Without even talking to my brother, I learned a lot from Mike

While living with my grandmother on 14 Hampton Ave, we had quite a few problems with the neighborhood kids. We would get into fights and altercations on a daily basis. In fact, we all had a separate set of enemies in Wilbur Section. Because it was four of us, many kids in the neighborhood would be so scared to fight us one-on-one that they would bring three or four extra kids to gang up on us. It got to a point that every time we left the street we had to take each other with us just to make sure we didn't get jumped.

On one particular day, we were out in the front of our grandmother's house playing. Mike and Steven were in junior high school and Charles and I were still in grammar school. Mike was playing on his ten-speed bike and we were playing touch football in the street. For a second, Mike's chain popped on his bike and he had to bend down to fix it. While he was bending over another kid was coming up the street on his bike. When the kid passed by Mike he cut the side of Mike's face with his bike pedal. The boy knew what he did but he just kept going. My brother got up real quick and didn't appear to be bothered too much by the hit despite how much he was bleeding. We all went into the house and he acted like nothing happened. He told my mother that the boy hit him by accident. He later told us when we were upstairs that the boy went to the same school. He then told Steven that he was going to get him back the next day.

The very next day, my brother and the boy who cut him with the bike talked and there was no altercation. They shook hands and left the situation right there. A few weeks went by and rumors started to spread in the neighborhood that the boy had punched my brother in the face and he didn't do anything. Some kids started to say that Mike apologized to the guy and told him that he didn't want any trouble. I remember some of the kids teasing my brother because they believed that he got snuck and he didn't defend himself. The dude was basically going around talking shit about it. We saw the boy a few times riding past our house but he never stopped. Out of respect for our grandmother's house, we never started trouble in front of her house. Things would always happen in school, at a park and of course at the Martin House.

One day we decided to play touch football in the alley around the corner from my grandmother's house. If we were all together, my mother would allow us to leave the front of the house. All of my brothers, a few of my female cousins and my friend Mike Green all decided to go. After about an hour, my brother saw the boy that hit him with the bike. He was walking down the alley with a few of his friends. When he got to where we were he started talking shit to my brother. He didn't talk directly to Mike, but he was talking loud enough for all of us to hear him. I could tell that my brother's mood changed because at first we were having fun. Now Mike had this serious look on his face. Mike didn't say anything at first. In fact, none of us said much at first. We were all waiting for Mike to give us the word. The boy walked up to Mike and started talking in his face. "Why did you lie about getting' hit in the face? Why you tellin' everybody that it was a mistake?"

Mike was confused because he really thought that this dude hit him by accident. Mike didn't answer him at first. Because Mike didn't answer him he kept talking shit to him.

"I should punch you in the face for real right now."

When Mike heard that I saw him get a little tense. He started looking around and started looking at us. There was three other guys with this dude and they were clearly too big for us. Mike was leaning on somebody's back porch with his hands behind him. He wasn't scared but I could tell that Mike was scheming. The rest of us were scared because we thought they were about to beat him up.

For some reason the guy kept talking to Mike. All of a sudden I saw Mike's left hand come up from behind him but he didn't have his fist balled up. From my angle it looked like he hit the guy on his shoulder. The guy started screaming like somebody shot him. Mike had thrown a hand full of dust that he had got off of the porch into the dudes eyes. He was blinded at that point and Mike just started punching him in the face. It looked like he hit him about six times before the guy fell. The other guys that were with him ran. They left him there. That was the first time that I saw Mike fight a dude that was bigger than he was. Now as a young kid, to watch my older brother defend himself even though he was out numbered was very liberating. I saw Mike overcome some of the biggest obstacles in his life. In turn, that gave me the confidence to use my heart and my abilities to overcome my own obstacles.

Steven

Of the four brothers, Steven is by far the most dynamic. And by dynamic I mean, he's complicated, borderline genius. Steven had a way of standing out. He was the trendsetter and the risk taker. He would think things, say things and do things that none of us would dare to think say or do. We all had a way of getting into our own trouble. There were always some issues that had to be addressed with us, whether it dealt with school, friends or family. But Steven was the one who would find a way to get *out* of trouble. Steve would always analyze the situation and see where he could take advantage of loopholes. Being that Steve was my older brother, I would learn a lot of tricks from him.

When Steve was in the sixth grade he had a paper route. We still lived on the west side of Trenton. Steven would make good money doing his paper route. He always had money for candy and money to buy toys from the corner store. We would play with these little green army men and Steven would have a lot of change to buy them. On a few occasions, Steven would let us accompany him on his paper routes to earn some change. He would always make us do all the work, especially when we distributed the Sunday papers, which had the most sheets. Those papers would get extremely heavy. Steven would carry the papers in a shopping cart and make us take the papers out of the carts and deliver them to the door. Steven always knew how to get out of work. As a bonus, Steve would let us come to his customer's house to collect on his route. This was good for us, because as he got the money we could be right there with our hand out to get paid for the week.

One night he decided to take us on his route to collect. Because it was late and it was also cold outside, he asked my father if he would drive us to the homes because it would be faster and we could get out of the cold. My father agreed and he drove us around. It was around Christmas time and the customers were tipping very well that night. They were giving him five and ten dollar tips. One lady even invited us in for some Christmas snacks. At first my father didn't want to stop, but he let us go in for a minute.

She lived in the Hilltonian section of Trenton. Walking into her house was like walking onto the set of the Cosby Show. She had a very large living room with an enormous Christmas tree. She had camel colored wall-to-wall carpet that ran throughout the house. There were about thirty wrapped gifts under a tree, which had all *white* candy canes on it instead of the normal red and white candy canes. I remember saying to myself that I wanted my house to look exactly like hers when I got older. She asked us to sit down in the living room while she went to the kitchen to grab some snacks. When she came back, she asked us where we were from and if were we enjoying the holidays. My brother Steven was very sociable but we didn't say much to her. It felt awkward, like we were not supposed to be in such a nice house. After about five minutes of eating and some small talk it was time for us to leave. She took our plates and went back into the kitchen. This time she was in the kitchen much longer than the first time. We all began to get restless. I remember looking at my younger brother Charles and he was laughing. Mike was definitely bored and Steven was simply waiting to get paid. They all were sitting on her couch and I was sitting on an armchair. Next to the armchair was a table that was adorned with glass animals. There were small horses, pigs and dogs that were made of glass facing in all directions. I saw them when I first came in but I started to pay more attention to them because we were waiting for so long. I picked up the dog. It was about the size of an action figure. But it was heavy. I started to pick up the horse when I heard a noise come from the kitchen. I thought the lady would be coming through the door but she didn't. After a few seconds, I picked up the horse. This piece was even heavier than the dog. My brothers were looking at me from the couch. When I looked over to them it seemed liked they were giving me the green light to be mischievous. Before I could even confirm the glances I put the horse in my pocket. As soon as I pulled my hand out of my pocket the lady was coming through the kitchen door. She had her purse in her hand. She gave my brother the money for the paper and a ten-dollar tip and told us all to have a good Christmas. We left.

When I got home I didn't even want the horse. I put the horse with all the other toys and didn't think anything of it. A few days later my father got a call from the lady. She told him that she was missing a piece of China from her table and she was sure that one of his sons took it. My father was immediately upset. He hung up the phone and came into our room. We were playing and immediately stopped when we saw him because we knew somebody was in trouble.

"Who the hell took the China?"

Nobody answered him. Partly because we didn't know what the hell a piece of China was.

"The lady invited y'all into the house and somebody stole from her. Who was it?"

Then it all came back to me. Damn. I was so scared that I couldn't even say anything. I knew what was going to happen if I told him that I took it. So I just stayed quiet. After about five minutes of getting no answer from us, my father decided to play dirty with us. He told us that we all would get a beating if nobody told him who stole the horse from the lady's house. At that moment, my brother Steven said that he took the horse. He said that he just wanted to see what it was and he didn't have time to put it back. He said he thought that if she saw him with it then she was going to think that he tried to steal it. He gave the horse back to my father. I thought he was going to get a beating for that but he never did. My father went and gave the horse back to the lady. I know Steven did it to protect me and I believe that he felt that my father would be harder on me than he would be on him. I never asked him why he did it, but it taught me a lesson about being loyal to my brothers.

Charles

Of the four brothers, Charles is the most creative. Charles is the self-starter. Being the youngest brother definitely gave him an opportunity to do his own thing. At the age of 13, he started working with the turntables and making music and he hasn't stopped making music since. My brother has been coming out with mixed tapes since he was 16. He would do the music, host the tape and design the cover all by himself. Like Steve, he would find the strangest ways to get out of trouble. If he was "on punishment" and couldn't use the phone, Charles would find a way to build a phone and talk on it. Because he is the youngest of the four, everyone looks out for him. Everyone in the family would rush to his aid if there were a problem. There were a few times that my older brothers would get into trouble if something happened to Charles when we were out.

Having a younger brother did have an advantage. Because of my little brother I was able to fly under the radar. He would get so much attention everywhere we went. Especially when we visited family. There were many lessons learned by having a younger brother.

In high school I had a best friend named Luis. Luis and I were really cool in junior high and for the first year of high school. We both lived in the southside of Trenton. He wasn't involved with my rap group but we were still close. I would always refer to Luis as part of the family because we were friends for a long time. His family clearly had more money than we did. His birthday parties would be at sports clubs and his mom would rent out arcades and invite the kids to his parties. But Luis was very "spoiled". During the first year of high school, my brothers, with the exception of Michael, saved up to buy a new basketball game for our Nintendo system. The game was called Double Dribble. It was a popular game and I was excited to have it. I told Luis about the game and invited him over to play with us. When Luis got there, he told us that he tried to get his mother to buy one for him but she told *him* that he had too many games. Because she wouldn't buy the game for him, Luis came by our house everyday for about a month to play.

One day my brothers and I came home and the back door was wide open. My mother was sitting on the couch and she was upset. She said it looked like someone broke into our house, but nothing was missing. We all checked our rooms but nothing was missing there either. After an hour or so of doing inventory on the house, Steven noticed that two

Nintendo games were gone-- Contra and Double Dribble. Now, we all are just as upset as my mother was because we already knew what happened. All of our friends and family knew that the back door was busted and that we kept it unlocked. I remember telling Luis that we had to get a new door but I didn't believe that he would come in and steal from our house. Ironically, a few days later, I was talking to Luis and he told me that his mother bought him the game. I just looked at him and didn't say anything. In the middle of our conversation I told him that somebody came in the house and took the game. He asked me if I knew who did it and I told him "no".

After talking to my brother Steven, he introduced a telling theory. He questioned, "Why would somebody just come and take the games and not the entire Nintendo?" After about a day, I went over to Luis' house and approached him about the game.
"Let me ask you a question. Did you take that Double Dribble game out of my house?"
"Hell no man. Why would I do that?"
"If you did it just tell me. I'll be mad but don't make it worse by lying."
"I swear to god that I didn't take your game. We are friends. Why would I do something foul like that?"
Luis sounded sincere so I dropped the conversation and left. I wanted to believe that he was my friend and that he would not do something like that. My brothers just kept pushing the issue. Charles was convinced that Luis was guilty because we all knew his mother told him that she wouldn't buy the game. And then a few days later he has the same two games

that were stolen from us. I didn't want to see it or believe that he would do something like that to us.

I went back over to his house about an hour later but he wasn't home. His mother was there and she told me that he went to the store. I took this opportunity to find out more information.

"I know Luis went to the store but I was coming by to get my Double Dribble game back."

"Oh that is yours. I was wondering where he got this one from. He kept asking me to buy him one but he has too many damn games."

I was so upset. I didn't even wait for him to come back home. His mother gave me the game and I left. I haven't seen his mother since that day. Reality hit. He actually came into my house and stole from me. I was so angry. The next day, I didn't say anything to him because I didn't know how to bring it up. I was hoping he would say something that would open the door for me to jump in. I remember sitting at the lunch table with another friend while Steven was sitting two tables over. Luis had an attitude because I wasn't saying anything to him. So I just came out and told him that I knew he broke into my house and stole the game. I also told him that I asked his mother if she bought the game and "no" was her answer. He denied stealing and said that he bought the game, not his mother. We got into this big argument and he threatened me. I stood up, he stood up and I swear before he could even raise his hands, my brother Charles was right there. Before I could even get a hit in, Charles slammed Luis on the table and that was it. The teachers snatched all of us and hauled us to the principal's office. We were all given a three-day suspension.

Charles was right there for me. He's down for whatever, any time, any place. I never have to worry about him having my back. We've always protected and helped each other. He's been a part of the same support team that helped us all along.

My grandparents:
Horace Smith (R.I.P.)
and Rosetta Smith ▶

◀My parents:
Joanne Taylor
and Michael Taylor

◀My mother with her four boys.

(L-R) Kenyatta, My Mother, Steven, Michael, Me and my cousin Simone is in the front.

◀Me @ 3 years young in front of my grandmother's house.

Me @ 5 years old graduating from the Head Start Program in Trenton, NJ.▶

◀Me, my brothers and my mother on christmas morning.

(L-R) Kenyatta, My Mother, Steven and Me.

◄My brother Mike right after he enlisted in the Army.

My brother Steven (extreme right) with his rap group.►

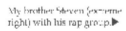

◄Me with my friend and my brother.

(L-R) Mike Green, Dashawn, Symphony

My brother DJ Symphony practicing on the turntables.►

▲ Me with some members of the New Poet Society. (L-R) Mc, Jah Shamel, Shabazz and Freedom God

◄My rhyming partner from the New Poet Society and our DJ.

(L-R) Babylee and Kevin "DJ Kashif" Robinson (R.I.P.)

◄ The infamous Trenton Makes, World Takes Bridge in Trenton, NJ

My photo I.D. for Community Service assigned by the PTI Program in Trenton, NJ ►

◄ My High School Graduation, Trenton Central High School,

7

The Five Percent Nation

For most of my childhood my mother tried her best to keep us in church. In fact, until I was about twelve years old, we would be forced to go to church on a regular basis. My mother wasn't a religious person but she felt that it was important for us to know God. She would make us go to Sunday school, then stay for the Sunday Service and even attend the evening sermons. I hated Sundays. And although none of us could sing to save our lives, my mother had us in the church choir. She wanted to keep us busy and active as much as she could. She figured she would rather have us in church then to have us in the streets. I never paid attention in church. None of us did. We were too busy laughing at other people in the church and being silly. Even when it was time to sing in the choir, we were always acting up and trying to make each other laugh. It was hard to take church serious because I just didn't believe in it. The music, the lessons and the people were not penetrating us at all. Instead of trying to grasp the message we were too busy asking ourselves why we had to put money in the collection plate when we were struggling to eat. There were a few times that my mother would give us a dollar each to put in the collection plate and we wouldn't put it in. We would keep the dollar and buy candy at the store. Sometimes I would even take the money back home and hide it until I got enough money to buy me a toy. I figured the money would do more good at home then leaving it with the church. When I entered the fifth grade my mother decided that it was time for me to get baptized. I got baptized in a pool that was located in the basement of the church. The reverend told me that I was going to be a new child. I remember getting nervous because I thought I was going to look different after the baptism. My mother told me that I would feel different and I would see things different but I would look the same. But after the baptism I didn't feel any different. In fact, besides the certificate that I got with my name on it, I was not affected by the whole ceremony. I think my faith in the church was lessened even more by the baptism because I expected so much but nothing happened. Another situation happened in the same church that made me question the true purpose.

False Idol

There were roughly about one hundred and twenty members in my church. My church would hold service in an old movie theater in Trenton. The building was very big and every Sunday it was crowded with people. The church was growing very fast. Reverend Wilson, who was our Reverend at the time, was very good and always found a way to keep the service entertaining. And although the message was not getting to me and my brothers, Reverend Wilson would preach the Word in a way that even the children could understand it. A few Saturdays of every month Reverend Wilson would have church picnics at his home in Ewing, NJ. His home was about 15 minutes outside of Trenton and was very nice. My mother would take us over there to eat and play with the other kids. One Saturday Reverend Wilson did not show up to the picnic. Mrs. Evelyn Wilson, his wife at the time, told everyone that he was sick and he couldn't make it. It was strange because this was his house and he wasn't around. About an hour later a young woman from the church, Ms. Pamela, showed up to the picnic. Ms. Pamela was a member of the church for a long time. However, she wouldn't make it to our service every Sunday. On a few occasions Reverend Wilson would even ask the church to pray for Ms. Pamela. On this particular day, Ms. Pamela showed up to the picnic with two young children. This was awkward because she never brought the children to church before. Everyone greeted her. She sat at the table with the grown-ups and the kids came over to where we were playing. It only took about fifteen minutes before things began to get uncomfortable around the picnic. Mrs. Evelyn was clearly upset with Ms. Pamela for coming to the picnic and no one could figure out why. They began to argue and a fight was close to breaking out. A few Deacons of the church tried to calm the situation down and begged for cooler heads to prevail. After a few minutes, Ms. Pamela grabbed the two children and left the picnic. No one was having a good time shortly after so my mother called a cab and we left the picnic.

Ms. Pamela didn't show up to church the next Sunday. Neither did Reverend Wilson. No one could figure out what was going on. Reverend Wilson did come to church the next Sunday and every Sunday following. Ms. Pamela didn't show and Reverend Wilson didn't ask anyone in the church to pray for her. In fact, no one in the church was even mentioning her name. About two months later Ms. Pamela did show up to church. She was obviously crying before she got there. She walked in the back door and decided to sit towards the back of the church. Everyone looked at her and became empathetic. But why was she crying? Did she get evicted? Did she have a death in the family? Reverend Wilson was clearly nervous and Mrs. Wilson was clearly upset. Towards the end of the service the truth came out. At the end of every service Reverend Wilson gave each member of the congregation an opportunity to tell the church what they were thankful for and what they were praying for. Usually my mother would stand up and tell the church that she was thankful for us and prayed that we would stay safe. On this day, however she did not stand up. A few people stood up and gave thanks. But everyone else was waiting for Ms. Pamela to stand up and tell of her troubles. Ms. Pamela did stand up. She even walked closer to the front of the church. But instead of walking all the way to the front she stayed in the center isle about four rows from the front. She closed her eyes, lifted her hands and began to speak.

"I have been living with a heavy burden in my chest for a long time. I want to ask God to lift it. I can't sleep at night, I can't go to work with my head high and I can't even come to church in peace. I want to ask God to forgive me for living in sin. I have been sleeping with Reverend Wilson for over five years now. I pray that he accepts his children, our children, as his own. Please Lord!"

There was a collective exhale in the church. A few people shouted praises and other people began to cry. It was like somebody bombed the church. Everyone was in shock. A few ushers rushed over to Ms. Pamela and they started to cry. The grabbed her and slowly walked to the back of the church. Mrs. Wilson stood up too and began to run to the back of the church. Before she could get to Ms. Pamela she was grabbed by a few Deacons. She began to shout at Ms. Pamela and call her a liar. Ms. Pamela was crying a lot now and telling everyone that Mrs. Wilson knew about the affair but never did anything to help her out. But before anything more could escalate Ms. Pamela was out the back door and gone. She never came back to church after that. Reverend Wilson began to lose member after member. My mother even pulled us out of that church and we started going to a church in Mill Hill. Although the incident was shocking at the time, it wasn't until a few years later that I fully understood what was going on. Reverend Wilson ended up moving the church to South Jersey. He started a new congregation and it became larger than the one he had in Trenton.

King Divine Cassien Born Allah

When I started middle school, my mother didn't stress us too much about going to church. She encouraged us to go but she began to use her Sundays to rest for her long work week. She was working two jobs and trying to find a new place to live. I went to church about once a month and made it to the Easter services. But towards eighth grade, I stopped going all together. I was no longer in the choir and really didn't see a point in going. I believed in God. But I didn't read the bible much and when I actually was in church I didn't pay attention. So I began to use my Sundays for rest too. As a got older, my attention span for church simply deteriorated.

During my freshman year in high school, I started hanging around a new friend. His name was Hakiem. He transferred to our school from a high school in New York City. As soon as he signed in our school he became very popular because he was from NYC. All the other kids were asking him how it was and what types of things he was doing up there. He was a cool dude but I could sense that he was into trouble. His father was a straight up Ol' G type and in his mid thirties. He was very different from my father. Although my father was a street veteran, he explained the importance of being successful. Hakiem's father would tell us to go out and enjoy our life. He would talk to us about girls and how to play them. He was more down to earth. So I started hanging around Hakiem real heavy. Hakiem was a rapper too. I was trying to make it as a rapper at the time so we quickly became tight. He would come to the studio with me and we would freestyle together. I introduced him to my brothers and they all got along. After a few months Hakiem started to bring these papers with him for me to read. He kept a large notebook with his *lessons* in them. Of course I didn't understand what it was because no one in my family was brought up Muslim. I did have one cousin who got locked up and when he came out he was Muslim but other than that, this was my first time being exposed to it.

Hakiem would bring his materials and explain what certain things meant but we weren't interested in him teaching us this religion. We told him that we were Baptist and that there was no need for us to learn his religion. But Hakiem was insistent and threw theories out at us and we clowned with him for a bit but after a while he stopped bringing his notebooks around. I'm always interested in learning new things but the Muslim religion wasn't one of them. One day I went over to his house. He lived about fifteen minutes away from us. His father told me that he wasn't there. He told me Hakiem was in a cipher. Hakiem's father was also heavy in The Five Percent Nation. So I left and headed back home. I passed a park and saw Hakiem and some other dudes in a circle. Being naïve, I thought they were rapping or something so I decided to go over to jump in. As I got closer I noticed that they were basically talking. I was loud as hell when I greeted Hakiem. All the other dudes looked at me like I was crazy and Hakiem had a serious look on his face too. I was about to turn around and walk away when they invited me to listen. I had to be quiet which was fine with me so I stayed and began to listen. They began talking again and it was like they were communicating in another language. That's where it became real intriguing to me.

Later that day, Hakiem and I talked about my converting over to The Five Percent Nation. He instructed me about how to get in and how to study. I would need to learn my lessons because I could be challenged at any moment. He continued to tell me that if I got caught out there not knowing my lessons that I would get physical justice. Physical justice was getting punched in the chest or the face for not knowing your lessons. A few days later he brought the lessons over and he said that he would teach me my lessons. I started learning my lessons and the first one I learned was the Supreme Alphabets. One day Hakiem came over and told me that he had a new name for me. He told me that Dashawn Taylor was my *slave name* and that I needed a new name to identify with my new knowledge of self. My middle name is Cassien and he basically told me that I was going to change my name to a Muslim name. Hakiem changed my name to King Divine Cassien Born Allah. Every part of my name had its own separate definition. Before I could learn anything else I had to learn what my name meant. When I was approached by another member of The Nation and he asked me to break my name down I had to know it word for word or I would get physical justice. I studied my lessons almost every day. After I learned my name I moved on to the Supreme Mathematics. From there I learned the Supreme Alphabets. I even mastered the 12 jewels of Islam. After I learned those lessons I would go out and build in ciphers to test my knowledge. We used to hook up with other Gods and

Earths and would build with them. A lot of the lessons taught me independence and discipline.

There were times where things got hard for me. But instead of praying to God, I would recite my lessons. The biggest thing in the Five Percent Nation is that you are God, you are the one. Allah means Arm-Leg-Leg-Arm-Head which symbolizes the human body. It's you. The Five Percent Nation was founded by Clarence 13X in 1964. The basic belief was that the black man is God and the Nation of Islam was teaching the people wrong. I remember a few times there were some people telling me that Elijah Muhammed, the leader of the Nation of Islam, and Clarence 13X had problems with each other and it caused a major division. When I heard that it kind of threw me for a loop.

A few things happened while I was in the Nation that was crazy. First, I don't think my mother ever knew that I was in the Nation because I didn't change the way I dressed or anything. My attitude changed a little bit but most importantly, my diet changed. I stopped eating pork and I haven't eaten pork since. I remember when I first got in the Nation; I had to fast for three days, while drinking vinegar only. I assume that was supposed to cleanse me. I'd never fasted like that before. That was another positive that I took away from it. Fasting for three days made me disciplined. My mother and grandmother still cooked pork and that caused somewhat of a problem. They questioned me about being too good to eat pork. And I told them no, it's just a filthy animal. The nation teaches you that a pig is a rat, cat and a dog mixed in one. I remember telling my mother that and she almost laughed me out of the house. I don't know if I really believed that but it was in the lessons. I stayed in the Nation for about eighteen months.

I had a cousin named Lynette. She was actually like a second cousin and she was into church. We would get into these discussions about the Nation. The one thing that Hakiem used to do was show us things in the bible what was contradictory and that was used to validate the Nation's lessons. I always wanted to learn and if something was contradicting I welcomed anyone who wanted to clear it up. Sometimes Lynette and I had heated arguments about religion. She would always question why I was in this new religion.

"So who told you that you were God?"

"God is the black man. He controls everything around him. Even the bible says that Jesus had black traits."

"That doesn't matter. If the black man is God and controls everything, why are black people so poor and always going to jail? Why can't they control that?"

Lynette and I would stay up late at night and argue back and forth. And although we both had good points, we were not budging in our beliefs. It was good to have these kinds of discussions because it opened my mind. It always made me question what I was learning. And although I was taking a lot of good information from the culture, I still had many questions that needed to be answered.

I was in The Nation for about six months when a few of my friends began to join in. They studied, got their new name and joined the ciphers that we were having at the high school. I helped them out as much as I could. But after about a year, I was the first one to get out. One particular cipher made me realize that this wasn't the religion for me. One of the guys in the cipher who was facilitating it began to speak about women. He said that the Muslim religion teaches us that the women can't worship with us. He continued by saying that between the teachings of the Muslim religion and the teachings of Clearance 13X, together he had a broad understanding of God and religion and that he would never have any dealings with women or allow them to tell him what to do. Now I was always raised to respect women and that didn't make sense to me. If the female was the earth, we needed them was my argument. He begged to differ and that's where I thought that teaching was man made because if God created everybody equal, which I believed as well, then how could we separate the two and create a hierarchy. That never sat well with me. Since then I questioned what the lessons were about. I found myself speaking out of turn in the ciphers, questioning what was said and that actually served as my exit out of it. I later realized that I took his teachings out of context. But instead of getting back into the religion I decided to keep the lessons and learn them on my own. I didn't participate in any ciphers and I dropped my new name. Being in the Five Percent Nation gave me a sense of self reliance. It forced me to think of my self as an independent being. It empowered me to stand on my own two and expect nothing from the world. And although I don't believe that I'm God, I do believe that I have access to his infinite knowledge and wisdom to do great things.

8
Hip-Hop

Those who are not into hip-hop will never understand the concept of getting bit by the hip-hop bug. I've been listening to hip-hop for over 20 years and there's nothing like it. It allows me to put my guard down and be myself. The first song that I ever heard in hip-hop was *Planet Rock*. I was at my cousin's house and that's the only song he played. I was only about five or six when I heard it. I was trying to understand what it was. It really didn't reach out and grab me the first time I heard it. It wasn't until I heard Slick Rick and Doug E. Fresh perform *"The Show"* that I was completely mesmerized by hip-hop.

We never played music in my house. I barely watched television because I was always outside. We only listened to the radio when we went to bed around eight or nine o'clock. The station we listened to back then was Power 99 out of Philadelphia. They would have the countdown at nine and *The Show* was #1 for almost two months straight. When I first heard the song I couldn't sleep. It exerted so much energy out of me. I tried to recite the song every night for those two months until I got them down. Before long every time I turned around somebody was singing it, that's how hot it was.

When I was eleven is when I really started buying hip-hop. I bought a walkman that had a tape player on it. Then I heard *The Bridge is Over*. It was so in your face and KRS-One's voice just drew me straight in. I heard the *King of Rock* on the radio and *My Radio* by LL Cool J and it was cool. But I was still just getting into it all together. But *The Bridge is Over* was in a class by itself. I remember buying the *Criminal Minded* tape with KRS One on the cover with a gun. That shit was so sexy to me. Young, black and in the hood, I wanted to be like that. Not necessarily with the gun, just taking no shorts. The culture snatched me up quick. I was writing rhymes at that time. And when I heard the first song on Criminal Minded, KRS One was killing it. It really just changed my life. To this day, I don't know what the hell I'd be doing without hip-hop because nothing else has ever had such a strong hold on me like hip-hop does. From the day that I heard *The Show*, my life has been one long rap song.

I've always wanted to get into the business and make money from it. And I always wanted to help push it to the next level. When I started listening to hip-hop in the mid-80's most people considered it a fad. They thought it would fade and some other music would replace it. Contrary to public belief, hip-hop raised me and that is the honest truth. While my father was in and out and I had real life issues, I tried to work those issues out myself through listening to music and taking the advice that I heard on the songs. I can't even explain it any other way. For example, *Jimmy* by Boogie Down Productions, reminded me to always protect myself from sexual diseases. My father didn't tell me about safe sex or even sex until a few years after I heard that song. In general, hip-hop helped me through life. There were a number of artists and groups that made a major impact on my life and the way I conducted myself.

KRS-ONE

My favorite MC when I was growing up. I say that because while hip-hop was on another page, KRS-ONE stayed on his own road. I actually didn't buy Criminal Minded when it first came out. I bought it after Scott La Rock got killed. When I bought it, I bought it specifically for The Bridge is Over. The first song on the album was Poetry. I kept rewinding it because I just couldn't get past the beat and the lyrics. They were so different from what I had heard before.

My cousin had LL's tape and when the video came out for *I'm Bad*, it didn't catch me. KRS-ONE pulled me in. Between *Dope Beat*, *Nine Millimeter*, and *Super Ho* was crazy with the slang and the beats. It was helping me expand my mind and it played as a different from of education to me. Once I started, hip-hop became addicted.

KRS-ONE was a huge inspiration to me from *Criminal Minded* to *My Philosophy*. I had to play the *My Philosophy* album so many times to understand what he was saying. His lyrics were so catchy and year after years he kept coming with the lessons. One of the major songs that really kind of had me on a whole different plane was *Why Is That*. When I heard that, it was around the same time I was getting into The Five Percent Nation. No rapper before that even remotely touched on political issues and church issues. When KRS-ONE did *Why Is That*, he started a lot of shit in my life. He quoted bible versus and broke down the tree from Abraham to Jesus. He was trying to prove that Jesus was black and basically bought the bible to hip-hop. It was explosive because I would take those verses and open up a bible. I was reluctant to read the bible when my mother sent me to church but hip-hop made me open the bible and study certain inconsistencies and questioning authority. Hip-Hop makes you question the status quo. It makes you buck the system and teaches you that there is no progress without resistance.

Another song that really stuck with me was a song he did called *Beef*. I believe this was in 1991 and he was talking about cows and how they put steroids in them. You can even see it today that our communities are bigger. Our children mature quicker and we attribute that to the eating habits. I stopped eating beef later though and I remember when I heard the song I thought it was so wild. Every one of his songs taught me something and I think a lot of it had to do with who he was and what he wanted to do. I don't know him personally but I could see that he had a serious bug to teach and he used hip-hop to translate his feelings and theories. When I was rhyming, half of me wanted to talk shit and the other side wanted to teach and give back more than just words like KRS-ONE did. By putting out songs like

Love's Gonna Get You and *Self Destruction*, his messages still remain with me today.

LL Cool J and Kool Moe Dee

I started following this battle in 1988. I'm not sure how it started. The first time I picked up on it I saw a video where LL was talking about Kool Moe Dee and it got me excited. The Bridge Is Over by KRS-ONE was cool to listen to but MC Shan didn't have much of a comeback. But the thing about the LL and Kool Moe Dee battle was that they went on for about four years. And that was really cool to me because I always thought that Kool Moe Dee was more lyrical than LL. To some, that's debatable but that's the best thing about hip-hop. For every fan that likes you there are two that don't, and vise versa. LL and Kool Moe Dee's battle was the art of the sport of lyrical jousting. It was something to listen to. And even though I didn't like LL, I bought his tapes to listen to his come backs to Kool Moe Dee. And it was the same for Kool Moe Dee. After a while, it got big and it pretty much died out when Kool Moe Dee couldn't make a record. LL was the bigger star and his fame defeated Moe Dee.

Big Daddy Kane

Big Daddy Kane came along as a part of the juice crew. He, in my opinion, made dark skinned nigga's cool again. Anybody growing up in the hood in the 80's knew that the guys that were getting all the girls were the pretty light skinned boys. The Ralph Tresvant types. Because of that Kane was a straight playboy. He made it cool to be dark skinned. The thing that people seem to forget about Big Daddy

Kane was that he was a lyrical rapper. I first heard him on *Ain't No Half Steppin'*. I started following him because he was really sarcastic with his delivery while others were beating around the bush. Kane was slick and off the wall with it. Kane made me see a new side of hip-hop. The verse that he did on *Lean on Me* was focusing on black power which demonstrated his diversity.

Poor Righteous Teachers

They hold a special place in my heart because they were from Trenton. I met Wise Intelligence and Culture Freedom in a few ciphers when they were living in Divine Land (the north side of Trenton). They were a part of The Five Percent Nation and that movement was growing. When they came out with *Rock This Funky Joint*, Trenton was on fire. It was hot for about two years and was playing on all the Philly radio stations. It was crazy because that's when everybody in Trenton thought they could rap. When PRT hit and they had the video with the Trenton Makes World Takes Bridge in it. The video was like a second coming. After the success of the first single and the video, PRT decided to drop a new single and shoot the video in Trenton. The next song was called *Easy Star*. Fliers circulated around the school telling how they were going to shoot Easy Star in the Mill Hill section of Trenton. I remember calling up my partners in my rap group and telling them to get ready because these dudes were going to put us on. I thought that nobody in Trenton could rap like us and knew we were about to get hooked up.

We went down to the video shoot and tried to talk to PRT. About 10,000 other people had the same idea. The park where they filmed the video was filled on both sides. It was flooded like they were doing a concert. When I saw that, it showed me how big hip-hop was and how big the movement was going to be. The people weren't there for a rally, they weren't there for a graduation, and they weren't there for church. They were there for PRT. Some hip-hop shit. This thing was bigger than us. I was thinking that we were going to go down there and there would be maybe 1000 people. I would be able to make my way to the front and talk to these dudes. But they were passing out the fliers and announcing it on the radio and people showed up from Philly, Camden, Willingboro and Atlantic City. It was crazy the amount of people who came out and I knew then that this hip-hop thing was going to be crazy. PRT indirectly helped pushed my mentality forward.

Once you get fans and can retain them, you would be set. That's how I felt and I give big shouts to Poor Righteous Teachers. They really made me believe that Trenton would do something. Subsequently, the second album didn't do too well. Wise Intelligence came out with a solo album that didn't do well. But the contribution that they made and the belief that they gave the people of Trenton was more than enough.

There were a couple of groups that spawned from that. Record labels started coming out to Trenton to see what was there. A group called Suicide Posse spawned, Big Beat Entertainment came out of Trenton and Boulevard Mosse even came out with a single. But the kings of Trenton were PRT. Poor Righteous Teachers made it happen.

EPMD

EPMD were, in my opinion, where ahead of their time. They actually made it cool to have a rap partner. Before then, most rap duos were very gimmicky and they were different personalities. When I first heard EPMD, here you had two MC's of the same caliber and they were making hot music. It was cool to see them together at the same time it made a serious impression on me. They sent the message that it was cool to have somebody else down with you and that solo shit may not always be the move. I didn't hear *Strictly Business* first, I heard *Unfinished Business* first and that's the one that I bought. The first song on there was So What You Sayin'. It was so hot that I couldn't tell which one was rappin'; they sounded so much alike. Immediately I became fans of theirs. At that time hip-hop was getting bigger. Another thing that I liked about EPMD was that they were one of the only groups who talked about making money. EPMD stands for Erick and Parish Making Dollars and this was during the time where black power was big. A lot of rappers were wearing medallions and wearing red, black and green. That was cool. Then you had EPMD stepping up talking about gold diggers and different shit. They were about moving records and getting certified. It was different than teaching about sex, money and drugs or making a better life for your selves. It was educational and inspired me. They were more like a money blueprint and I have to credit them on the group mentality that they represented.

NWA

Niggas With Attitude. The first time I heard NWA was when I was around thirteen years old. Mike Green introduced me to NWA and I thought that KRS-ONE was bad with the gun on the cover. The first song I heard from NWA was Straight Out of Compton. Mike and I were walking to the store. Mike was never a rapper and all of a sudden he breaks out rapping.

"*You too boy if you mess with me the police are gonna have to come get me off your ass that's what I'm talking bout.*"

I listened to him and was shocked. I was like 'did you write that crazy shit'? He told me that was Ice Cube. He told me that he was in a group called NWA. We went back to his house and he played their tape for me.

Listening to NWA was like looking at a dirty magazine back then. I didn't tell anyone about it. I bought it from Sound Express in downtown Trenton. I took it home and played it. That was the first time that I heard a rapper talking about actually killing somebody. Some rappers talked about being the baddest dudes around but it wasn't murder music. It was also the first time where I heard women referred to as bitches. At 13 years old and when you hear that, it sounds crazy. I listened to the music more and more and it too became so addictive. Because of the type of stuff they talked about, I didn't listen to it out in the open. I always wore my headphones. Even like a year later, they came out with a song called *She Swallowed It*. The title is self explanatory and so far out of the ordinary for me. With this song, I actually thought the chick was giving oral sex right there. It's hard to explain the emotions and feelings that I had when I listened to this music.

Listening to East coast rap and West coast was different. For example, East coast rap was more lyrical. It expressed a love for music. The West Coast Rap was more gangster. All of west coast music evoked more angry emotions in me. It was so vulgar and rough at the time. Again, I can't explain how confused I was when I heard skits during the record. I would hear gun shots and screams and I really thought that was happening right there. That's how the music had my mind. I was almost brain washed. One day when I was sixteen, I heard this song called *Fuck the Police*. It was a very popular song. My father wasn't living with us at the time but he happened to come over that day. Now normally when he dropped by when he wasn't living with us, somebody was in trouble. But this time he just wanted to stop by and check on us. My father heard me listening to the song and he basically told me to throw the tape away. I didn't even ask him why. All he said was to throw it away and that I better not listen to that crap anymore. I remember not throwing it away despite the fact that I told him I would. I knew he was angry that I was even listening to that type of music. I was getting older and becoming a little rebellious. I was addicted to the West coast rappers. I bought all of Ice Cubes music, The Chronic, DoggyStyle and even MC Ren's tapes. The way they were bringing it was overwhelming as a young kid and to this day I couldn't tell you whether this was good or bad. It definitely made me lack respect in certain woman. It was angry music so it didn't put me in the best of moods when I listened to it. On the flip side it did make me put to question the status quo. It helped me grow up and see the world in its realest form as opposed to a fairy tale place that's full of joy. The world is ugly and these rappers put to light what's done in the dark.

Naughty by Nature

Naughty by Nature was a classic New Jersey Group. They came out when I was in high school. I remember the first time I heard Treach's style. He was dope to me. Treach was a fast rapper. He had crazy metaphors and was very unorthodox. If you closed your eyes and listened to different rap songs, you could pick up on his individuality and not mistake him for anybody else. He was clearly in left field doing his own thing on his own accord. To me Treach really put New Jersey rappers on the map. He was competing with other lyricist from New Jersey like Redman and Queen Latifah. But then he dropped *OPP* and it was over. *OPP* was hip-hop slang that transcended outside the hood. That's when you knew the song was big. Once Run DMC did *My Adidas*, everybody could relate and they got big. And the same thing with *OPP*, Other Peoples Property, it was a killer. I first heard the song when I went to a club called The Electric Playground. It was a club for teenagers and you didn't even have to show ID to get in. I went in and Naughty by Nature was actually performing. Treach came out with no jewelry. All he had on was a metal chain with a lock on it. They all had baseball bats on stage and that to me was hip-hop. They were straight street. When Treach did the song from Juice, *Uptown Anthem* the beat made the crowd go crazy. I never heard the song before. That was a trend for Trenton. We were always late getting music. Treach was young and his flow was somewhere else. The way he flowed, his delivery and the subject matter that he talked about got me really hyped to step my game up. When I found out that they were really from Jersey, I was floored. It really didn't matter to me which part of Jersey you were from. If you made it as a rapper and were delivering it ungodly, then you were family. New York, Los Angeles and Philly had such a strong hold on hip-hop. And to have one of the biggest hip-hop songs of all time be put out by someone from Jersey was crazy. I bought all of their albums too. I was a big fan of Treach for a long time because Jersey finally had a lyricist that was tight enough to hold his own. I have to tip my hat to him because what Poor Righteous Teachers did for Trenton, Treach did for Jersey as a whole.

The Wu Tang Clan

The Wu Tang Clan hit the streets right before I graduated High School. I remember my older brother bringing this tape home. It was in this white box. It had a sword on the box and had Wu Tang Clan on it in black letters. On the other side it had a solo song by Method Man. When my brother came home he just threw the tape at me and told me that he picked it up from downtown and that it was mine. Apparently they were giving out these tapes down there. I took it and put it to the side. The cover of the tape reminded me of the Fu-Schnickens. I didn't want to hear another rap group that was on that chop suey shit.

One day when I was bored out of my mind, I decided to play the tape. I was walking to school and popped it into my walkman. The name of the song was *Protect Ya Neck*. It normally took me about forty minutes to get to school but this day I think it took me about two hours because as soon as I heard the song I had to stop to listen to it over and over again, it was so incredible. Every single artist of the Wu Tang Clan had a different style and the tape hit me like a comet. I could not even tell you what was in front of me as I was walking because I was so engrossed in the song. They were the crack of hip-hop to me at the time. I don't think a song ever had that much of an impact on me since *The Bridge is Over*. I kept rewinding the tape over and over again. Each verse and MC was like a ride. It was in your face talking about the Gods and Earth and since I was already in the Nation before, I knew what they were talking about. The song was completely different from how they marketed the song on the tape. It was a thousand times better than how it was presented on the cover. The *Protect Your Neck* song hit me so hard from the first time I heard it. I still think the GZA's verse is one of the best finishes ever.

This was the early 90's and Wu Tang was rapping about shit that you only heard on the West coast and I started following them and getting to know who they were. To me Wu Tang was the biggest movement in hip-hop ever. Wu Tang killer bees were always with them, groups of them, no rappers just killer bees. And anyone living on the East Coast from '92-'98, knows what I'm talking about. There were a lot of movements that blew up after Wu Tang: Rough Riders, G-Unit, NWA, Cash Money Click and even State Property. But the street presence of Wu Tang for me had to be the biggest I had ever seen in my life. I can honestly say that if I lived in Staten Island or North Jersey I probably would've been a killer bee myself. The whole crazy part about the Wu Tang was that all of the MC's were able to stand on their own. All eight of them were able to do solo projects because they were so different from the next rapper. And this was in total contrast from what EPMD was giving us before. They were two different rappers but sounded the same. Now you were talking about eight MC's with eight different personalities that they all were delivering. To me that was remarkable.

I would rewind the songs back tens of times just so that I could learn the words and keep them in my head. I don't know why my brother gave me the tape but I'm glad he tossed me one. It turned out to be a bag of crack because I was so addicted from the time that I popped it in. I always respected Rza for putting that whole thing together. They showed me a different side of hip-hop and put a stamp on the whole hip-hop movement thing.

From top to bottom, Hip-Hop is the basis of who I am today. The good and the bad. The sense of community, the sense of hustle and the sense of education all comes from the boom bap. Sometimes I try to imagine my life if hip-hop didn't exist. It's so scary that I try not to dwell on it too long. And only those that are into the culture will only understand the true nature of the beast.

9
New Poet Society

As I moved into my first year in junior high school, I made up my mind that I wanted to be successful. But I just didn't want to graduate high school and get a good job. I wanted to do big things. I was fascinated by the entertainment industry and even more fascinated by hip-hop itself. After hearing rap songs for the first few years I found myself writing rhymes of my own and battling people just for fun. But as I got older I became more serious about my entertainment career. I begged my brother Steven to be a part of his rap group but I was too young. He was getting his rap skills up and I was still playing around with it. I decided to start a solo career and I asked my best friend Mike Green to be my DJ. In the beginning things looked as if we could get a record deal and I would be able to get out of Trenton. One particular situation taught me a serious lesson on the rap game.

Radio Waves

Mike Green and I never had a name for our rap group. I was using the name MC Double D and he was using DJ Mike G at the time. I was staying in the Mill Hill section and he lived on E. State Street in Wilbur section. I used to go over to his house and watch rap videos. While the videos were playing I would write some rhymes and kick them to the beats. Mike didn't even have turntables. He just had an old record player. We would talk about our dreams of making it big in the industry.

One day we were sitting on his front porch. I was flipping through my rhyme book and Mike was just hanging out. Out of no where this guy comes up to us and starts talking with us. He had on a blue and white Adidas sweat suit. He wore a furry bucket style Kangol hat and he was wearing a large gold rope. He had a pair of black shades in his hands that were flooded with gold rings. He didn't look like he was from the neighborhood. He looked like he fell out of Crush Groove. He walked up on the porch and started talking to Mike.

" Wassup G. Y'all a rap group?"

"You know it. I'm Mike G and this is my partner Double D. He's the rapper."

"Okay, okay. I'm Lee. I manage a few rap groups. Y'all got a manager?"

"Nah"

"Well if you want I can get you on the radio tonight. I worked with Chuck D, Wise Intelligent and even Queen Latifah."

When he told us that he could get us on the radio I became really interested. I use to hear songs on the radio and I knew that I would shine if I was on the radio saying some of my rhymes. I didn't know who he was so I wasn't totally sold. He started telling us about his studio that he had.

"Tell you what. Come over to my studio and I'll let you listen to some of my artists."

We didn't have anything to do so we agreed. His studio was down the street from Mike Green's house so we didn't have to go far. When we got to his house he started looking for his keys. He shuffled around for a minute and told us that he lost his keys and had to wait for his partner to get back. We sat on the porch and talked about rapping and the music industry. He invited us to go to a radio station, WPRB in Princeton. He told us that he could get us right on the air. He planned on taking us to the radio station that very same night. We just met this dude and now he was talking about taking us to the radio station. He wanted us to meet him in three hours on the porch and we needed to look good.

"Meet me back here tonight and make sure y'all got matching suits on."

"Why?"

"Because y'all have to look like a rap group."

"Well we don't have any suits."

"Well I can buy the suits for y'all. They are $25.00 each. I will get the suits, you just have to pay me back."

At first I didn't like the idea of giving him any money. But I wanted to get on the radio very bad. I was excited and really believed that I was going to get a record deal. I walked back home and Mike went home to ask his mother for money. Here I was 13 years old asking my mother for $25.00. My mother wanted to know what Lee was talking about. She always supported what I did and listened to what I had to say. So I explained the situation. I told her that we'd just met him and he told Mike and I that he would to take us up to the radio station but we needed to get our gear right. She agreed but only had $15.00. It was her last $15.00 and she gave it to me.

I walked back over to East Trenton and it was late by now. On the way I stopped by my grandmother's house and told her what was going on because I was so excited. I felt like it was about to happen for me. I was about to be a star. I asked her for the remaining $10.00. My grandmother told me that she didn't have it. So my uncle was there and he gave me the $10.00. Needless to say, I was so excited. I thought it was about to go down.

I went down to Mike's and when I got there, he said that his Mom's only had $15.00. Mike was concerned with what this guy Lee was going to say. We had $40.00 between us. Supposedly he'd already bought the suits. Mike asked me about the radio station and did I hear anything about us being on the show.

"You know WPRB usually plays hip-hop music on Thursday nights."

The problem was that it was Wednesday. We waited on the porch for Lee. He pulled up in the car with this guy with him. Lee got out of the car and came over to us. He asked us for the money for the suits. I told him that we only had $40.00. He gave me a disappointed look but he took the money and said we could pay him the $10.00 when we become big stars. He took the money and told us that he would run and get the suits and that he'd be back to pick us up later. We waited on the porch for him to come back.

Unfortunately, that was the last time we saw Lee. We talked for about an hour on Mike's porch and Lee never showed up. We decided to walk down to his studio to see if he was there. Mike was upset and started to piece it together.

"He didn't even have our sizes. How is he gonna get the suits for us? And WPRB is not playing hip-hop music tonight. I think he got us."

I still didn't want to believe that this man Lee took our money. I kept looking for his car as we walked but I couldn't remember what it looked like. I did however remember what his face looked like. When we got to the house we rang all the doorbells. We didn't know which apartment he lived in because he never actually went in. We knocked and finally this little girl came out. We asked for Lee and she told us that no one by the name of Lee lived there. Upset and disappointed we started to knock on all of the doors. But everyone told us that he didn't live there. Reality hit and our world came crumbling down. This dude had played us out and we couldn't believe it. I remember sitting on Mike's porch late at night and was like damn! I was so hurt. I wasn't crying but I was mad as hell because it was like I just knew this was it. This was how I was going to get everybody out of the hood. I thought this was my opportunity of lifetime.

When I got back home, it was late and my Mother was mad because I was supposed to be in the house before it got dark. When she looked in my face she saw that something was wrong. She asked me if I'd gone to the radio station. I just said no. She didn't ask me anything else. I went from having a feeling of triumph and success to the feeling of being a loser in less than two hours. I was stressed out. Today I can laugh about it but at the time, I was crushed. Things were too good to be true and that's where I get a lot of my cautiousness from. I'm always looking out for that boulder to clobber me in the head and let me know that it's not going to go as smoothly as it appears to be going. I'm thankful however for that experience because it taught me a lot.

As for Lee, when I was in high school Mike called me and said that he saw this Lee's picture in the paper. He was shot and killed in West Trenton. I never found out the details behind his death. A few people in Trenton knew of him and always knew that he played dirty.

Birth of NPS

I never let the Lee situation get me down. I always wanted to break into the entertainment industry and I kept writing rhymes. In the eighth grade I turned up my love for hip-hop. I wanted to start a rap group so I started searching for rappers to be down with. As fate would have it I ran into a female rapper one day at a talent contest in Downtown Trenton. Her name was BabyLee. She was very good with the lyrics and she had great stage presence. We went to the same junior high school together but I never paid any attention to her because she lived on the north side of Trenton. After talking for a few weeks she told me that she started a group called The New Poet Society but she recently lost her only partner. So I immediately moved in the vacant spot and we started the group. As we moved into the ninth grade we started to really take off with the idea. We started to record songs at her mother's house. Her mother had some industry ties so that made it easier. As our name got stronger around Trenton we began to recruit other rappers. My brother Steven even joined the group after his crew split up. Before you knew it, we had about 12 members all together in The New Poet Society.

BabyLee and I were basically the heads of the operation. We started to run the rap group like a business. We would have meetings and try to figure out ways to make money and at the same time, promote the name. My close friend at the time Jah Shamel was the first additional rapper to come on board. Montique (my older brother) joined about six months later. My younger brother, DJ Symphony joined in as one of our djs. Shabazz, who rapped and sang at the same time, was added around the same time as another rapper named Freedom God. Then we had Mike Green who did reggae and went by the name of General Mike. We had another DJ, DJ Kashif, (RIP). He lived in the same neighborhood in south Trenton. We had an older guy join the group also. His name was Lucent. This guy was incredible. He was one of the last rappers to come on board. His rap name was Sunstar. Then there was E. Power. He rapped and did a little reggae also. He was down for a minute. We had my man Hakiem. He was the one who got me into the Five Percent Nation. So our group consisted of ten rappers and two DJ's. All throughout high school, we battled other groups. We won some and lost some of course but the movement was so big that we started running into a lot of problems.

Rap Beef

It was the summer between my sophomore and junior year in high school. At that time we were doing two shows a month in the Trenton area. We also hit Pennsylvania a few times. We weren't putting out music though. There weren't any mixed tapes out there on the streets. It was more like we were trying to get a record deal and get in contact with the right people. We were basically doing shows and really trying to blow up. We did a show at Junior 2 on the East side of Trenton at an event called World Day. It was a showcase that we got paid to do and it was a program that I had worked with the staff to facilitate. I was trying to get us money any way I could. I wasn't living in Wilbur Section at the time. There were only two of the group members living in East Trenton. Baby Lee lived on the North side along with Freedom. Shabazz, General Mike and Jah Shamel lived out in East Trenton. I was out of South Trenton along with my brother and Sunstar.

When we went to do the show at World Day, there was another group there by the name of The Kingdom. It was about 8 people in the group. They were real thugged-out and all of them were in The Five Percent Nation. I remember them going first and doing a song that had the word "Nubian" in it and they had a lot of people in the crowd that were feeling them. Then we did a song called *Proud to be a Nubian* and it caught fire quick. A few people had it on tape already from when we recorded in the studio. It was a huge hit. The people were singing along with us. It was me, Montique, General Mike, DJ Symphony and Sunstar. After we did the song, we did the normal shakes, got off stage and immediately we started getting dirty looks from The Kingdom.

Shortly there after, we got a call from General Mike and he told us that a lot of people were talking about us on the streets. The group The Kingdom felt that we bit their song and they started talking shit. They had a little power on the streets. We didn't know what their song was about. All we knew was that the word Nubian was in the hook. So Mike had suggested that I speak to one the dudes from the group.

Knowledge was the member of the group that Mike wanted me to talk to. He was a pretty cool dude. He had known my brother Symphony from a few parties in Trenton. So I went to meet with him and when I met with him he was still cool. He asked me about the song and told me that his producer was angry. They were making moves and closer to getting a deal than we were and that was an issue. I told him that Sunstar hit us off with the song and that we weren't trying to bite, we were trying to make things happen. After we talked he and I kind of hit it off. He was cool with how I told him the song was developed and we left it alone. Two days later, Mike called me again and told me that there was some serious beef going on. Apparently another member of the group named Black was upset that I didn't speak to him about the beef. We saw him at a high school party and we didn't speak to him. He felt that I snubbed him and he was upset. Mike went on to say that The Kingdom was tripping and when we see them again, we were going to have some problems. With that information, I scheduled a meeting. That was the first time that the power structure was defined in the group. Baby Lee was there and she was listening to us. Nobody really knew what to say or do and I came up with the idea of coming up with a song dissin' The Kingdom. The purpose was to let them know that we weren't scared of them. Baby Lee wasn't cool with my idea and decided she was out. Everyone else agreed so we went forward with the plan. A couple of weeks went by and nothing really happened. One day my brother called over to the house. He had told me that he was over at our grandmother's house and he saw that dude Black at the store. He tried to break out and get his boys and when Symphony came out of the store, they were looking at him real crazy. They were trying to intimidate us and I wasn't feeling that. So without the blessing of Baby Lee, I called Mike and told him that we needed to do this soon because this situation was getting a little bit serious. There was a block party being thrown by the Martin house and an estimated 500 people were supposed to be there. Mike and I sat and talked for about an hour and decided to do a song called *Warning Shot*. The message to them would be for them to chill. We were watching them just like they were watching us and we're deeper than they thought we were. So Mike came up with the hook. Everybody wrote versus and we came up with the song.

The Kingdom was schedule to perform that day as well. I don't believe they were aware that we grew up in the Martin house and that we knew the coordinators. I arranged for us to go on after The Kingdom. That was a must. They obliged and switched the order. BabyLee decided not to come to the show. She figured it was probably going to get violent and she didn't want any part of that. We arrived at the block party about two hours before we were to go on and The Kingdom was there. They were deep but we were deeper. We had people who were just down for us and not necessarily in the group. The Kingdom went up and did their song. Ironically the song was called the Dead Poets Society. The Kingdom was definitely coming at us and wasn't going to back down. Right after they got off of stage, I ran up and grabbed the mic. I addressed the beef with The Kingdom and the problems that people thought existed. I told them that there was no problem.

"This is about Hip-Hop. Rap groups will come and go but there will only be one Society left when this beef is over. "

I was talking mad shit. We started the show without a beat. We just started addressing all of the members of The Kingdom. The crowd was going crazy. We were hyped and still talking shit. Everybody got there verse off and the set was over. There was a little commotion after we did our song. Black told me that he was going to see me soon and just walked off. There wasn't an altercation that day and I didn't think anything of the situation.

As my junior year began the problems with The Kingdom began to mount. We would see each other in the hallways and have small fights but nothing major. Black dropped out of high school during my junior year so I never saw him in school. I did run into him at a party in South Trenton. DJ Kashif was throwing a party in the Kingsbury Projects in South Trenton. It was a block party for his building. I knew there were two members of The Kingdom that lived in the Kingsbury Projects but I wasn't worried about them. I wanted to go to support DJ Kashif. When I got to the party I saw Kashif setting up his equipment and went to say what's up to him. After about an hour Black came into the park. I started to leave because I was alone but something told me to stay. As soon as Black saw me, he walked up on me and starts talking shit.

"What the hell are you doing here?"

"Who the hell are you the security guard?

I had a drink in my hand. When I reached over to put it down but before I could come back up one of Black's friends came from my side and punched me in the face. Then Black grabbed me from the front and tossed me over the park bench. They were all on me trying to punch me and stuff. I rolled under the bench and that saved me. Kashif came over and pushed the dudes off of me. Now I was pissed. It was four of them against me.

I left the party and called Mike and told him what happened. He called his brothers and we went back down there. Before we got there, Mike told me that he wanted to go in the park first to see if they were still there. As we approached the gate I saw that all of them were still down there. Before Mike could even grab me I ran over there and punched Black right in the face. We were fighting and people started jumping in but Mike was right there to stop that. He was letting Black and I get it in. Black was smaller than me and I was giving it to him. After I got him on the ground I began to kick him and Mike came over and pulled me off and it was over. It was a serious beat down.

When I got home, I told my brothers the story and to watch their backs. The situation had escalated so fast. A few months after that, Jah Shamel had gotten jumped and robbed as he walked home one night. We weren't sure if it was The Kingdom that did it. We'd see these same dudes at a party and it would be eight of them and maybe one or two of us. We'd have to leave. And sometimes it would be the opposite where as there were more of us than them. It was all over hip hop. But the problems with them would soon boil over.

10
Broken Promise

As I approached my senior year in high school things were getting very complicated in my life. I was working full time, I owned my own business, I was trying to make it to college and my problems on the street were mounting. People were calling my house threatening me and most of my friends were fighting continuously with The Kingdom rap group. I decided to try to peace things up with a few members of the other rap group before things spun out of control. But before a meeting could ever get setup the beef escalated.

Show me Yours and I'll Show You Mines

One afternoon, I decided to head out to a concert in North Trenton. The city was holding the annual carnival in the fair grounds behind Donnelly Homes. K-Solo had come to town to perform and I decided to see him perform. No one from NPS was around so I decided to hang out with my cousin Tony. Tony lived in East Trenton and he agreed to walk over to the carnival with me. The show was hot and K-Solo tore down the place. However, his performance was cut short by a fight in the crowd. The show was over and everyone began to clear out the fair grounds. While we were walking out of the carnival I spotted a few of the guys from The Kingdom. Black wasn't with them. I looked over to them to see if there was going to be a problem. They saw me and one of the dudes walked over to me.

"Ain't you from NPS?"

"Yeah, why?"

"I don't know why you are over this way. This could be bad for you."

"Yeah, well I guess it's going to be bad for me." It was almost like a warning and I think he wanted to see what we were going to do. My cousin Tony was a lot more *street* than I was. He basically told him that we weren't going anywhere. My heart started pumping really fast. They had more than two with them and I just knew it was about to get cracking. They walked off and we stayed around for a minute. I wanted to leave at first but Tony didn't really have any fear. He just wanted to stay to make sure we were good. About a half an hour later we decided to leave. As we approached the Southard Street Bridge we heard somebody yelling. I couldn't tell who it was but they were telling us to wait. They were too far for us to see who it was. I didn't want to wait but Tony did. So we waited and it was the same dudes from the carnival. They ran up on us and one of the dudes starts talking to Tony.

"Didn't we tell y'all to get out of this neighborhood?"

"What are you talking about? Y'all don't own this block!"

And before Tony could say anything else the dudes pulled out a gun. That was the second time I had a gun pulled on me and that was some scary shit. He pointed the gun right at us. The guy starts to yell at Tony.

"Now take off ya chain and give it to me."

Tony took off the chain and gave it to him. The dude took the chain and basically told us not to come back through there again. Then they walked off. Tony was mad as hell. I told them that the only reason why he took the chain was because he thought you were down with NPS. Tony wasn't even listening to me. He kept saying that he thought about getting a gun and now was the perfect opportunity. I remember feeling nervous because I knew I had to travel in North Trenton and I was still trying to get a record deal for NPS. I didn't have a car so I had to walk everywhere. Tony told me that I needed to get a gun too. I didn't want to do that. I would rather take my chances and fight before I carry. Tony ended up going his way and I went mine.

A few weeks later I got a call from my cousin and he told me that whenever I can to come by the house. He didn't tell me why. He said he needed to talk to me. I went there after school one day and Tony showed me a gun. And surprisingly, he had one for me to. When he handed me the gun I didn't want to take it. But a part of me wanted to protect myself. He told me to put it somewhere safe so that I'd have it if I ever needed it. I was a little nervous. I wasn't nervous about having the gun. I was more nervous about getting caught with it. I was scared that I may have had to use it. That was my biggest fear. I quickly put it away in my book bag.

For about four months, I hid the gun in my house. My room was in the basement and it was easy to hide it down there because no one came down there. I only took the gun out the house once. I went to a party down at the Masonic Temple. The Temple was located right in the center of town. It was teen night. I was going to the party with my friends but I wanted to protect myself in case I ran into The Kingdom. My cousin Tony was going to be there so Jah Shamel and I went together. I felt fearless and was almost begging these dudes to run up on us. A crazy sense of power came over me. I was nervous and confident simultaneously. When we got to the party we weren't even frisked. They didn't check for weapons or anything. Around 12:00 the party was over. As I was walking home I became upset because I didn't see those dudes from North Trenton. I didn't really want to hurt anyone; I just wanted to show them how it felt to have a gun pointed at them. That wasn't a good feeling because now I wasn't scared to carry it. That to me was a downfall. I never saw any of the dudes from The Kingdom while I had the gun on me. It never dawned on me and I never took into account that they could've been carrying guns too and that somebody could get seriously hurt.

Poetic Justice

Things really calmed down during the last half of my senior year. I was looking to graduate high school and get on with my life and try to make some big things happened. I got an acceptance letter to college in March and was excited about that. I was finally going to move out of Trenton and start doing some serious business now.

During spring break, I decided to visit my cousin Tony. I wanted to give him his gun back. I really didn't have a use for it. Things calmed down with The Kingdom and we ran into them less frequently. When I got to his house he was sitting on his porch and another guy was sitting on his stairs. I handed my cousin the book bag with the gun in it and told him that I didn't need it. Tony just looked at me and didn't say anything. Instead of leaving and going back home, I decided to chill for a minute with them. I walked off the porch and sat on somebody's car that was parked on the curb. Then things got stupid.

My cousin looked in the bag and grabbed the gun. He asked me did I even fire it and I told him no. So my cousin pointed the gun in the air and let off a shot. It was so loud that it hurt my ears. I saw a few people down the street look up and then went back to their business. In his neighborhood gunshots were not a big deal. Luckily no one was home at his house. About fifteen minutes later I was looking down the street and noticed a cop car driving slowly up the road. He was moving slow and his lights weren't on so I didn't think anything of it. Then I looked to my left and there was another cop car moving slowly. Then I started talking to myself.

"Damn they are about to roll on somebody-"

Before I could get another word out I heard a loud bang. It wasn't a gunshot. It was the opening of the police car door. The cops began to yell for everybody to put their hands up. I looked over to the cop on my left to see who he was yelling at. When I looked back over to my right I was staring down another barrel of another gun. Now this is the third time I had a gun to my face and I wasn't even eighteen yet. I threw my hands up as I asked what was going on. About eight other cop cars came from around the corner. The other dude broke out and my cousin was still on the porch. They began to ask us where the gun was and I told them that I didn't have one. They grabbed my cousin, threw the cuffs on him and put him in the car. They turned me around and begin to frisk me. I tried to tell them that I didn't have a gun on me. Instead of putting cuffs on me they threw me in the back of the paddy wagon. Before they grabbed my cousin, he put his gun in my book bag. I saw them looking around on the porch. They located the book bag and got back in the car. Instead of taking us straight to the police station they were driving around Trenton. They took us the long way. My cousin and I were sitting in the back looking at each other. I was thinking why was he shooting the gun off and he's looking at me like it was my fault. We thought they were just trying to scare us or something but shortly thereafter we were at the police station.

They took me out of the truck and brought me into the station. They sat me on the bench and automatically took my cousin to a different room altogether. Then a cop came and handcuffed me to the bench. He asked me questions.

"Why did you have a gun?"

"I didn't have a gun?"

"Who's gun is it?"

"I don't know what you are talking about. I never saw a gun."

The officer told me that I was going to be charged with possession. They finger printed me and put me in a holding cell. I was locked up on gun charges when I didn't have one. They took all of my belongings and identification. I was worried that they were going to call my parents. My father always told me that if I ever got locked up not to call him because he wasn't coming to get me. Shortly thereafter, they took me to the county. I wasn't officially charged and no one had read me my rights. No one questioned me or anything. I had to stay the night in the county. Getting locked up and not knowing anything was crazy to me. I thought I was really about to go down. I was scared shitless. I couldn't believe that all of this was happening right before the summer. I was looking forward to going to college and making big things happen.

I was released after three days. On the third night they let me out on my own recognizance. I thought it was over at that point and made no mention of it to any of my family members. I kept it to myself because I didn't want it to get crazy. My parents were happy that I was on my way to school and I didn't want to disappoint them. A few days later a letter came to my house. It was a pre-trial intervention letter. The charges were weapons possession. My court date came and they asked me about the particulars of the case. I told them that I didn't have a weapon and told them what happened when the cops came. They ended up charging me with weapons possession. But because it was my first offense I had to sign PTI papers and do community service.

I remember thinking that I couldn't go down this road. I was so happy that it was my senior year because I was leaving for college just in time. I knew things were going to escalate because I had issues with dudes that wanted to take it to another level. The few days that I spent locked up made me look at my decisions with a microscope. I could've ended up dead doing that bullshit. Would I have used the gun? I don't know. But I do know if it came down to it, I would have defended myself. Getting arrested became the lesser of two evils and justice was served. A few years later New Jersey changed their state law on gun possession. I could've got 3-5 years if I caught a charge. If I was still there, never having gone to college, who knows what would've happened.

For the first 18 years of my life I have been trying to escape this city. I never wanted to live a life of poverty, lack and limitation. I made a promise to myself at a very young age that I would escape Trenton. Did I keep that promise? Absolutely not! I am Trenton. The everyday hustle, the will to do better and my resilience all comes from Trenton. I am physically away from my home but my entire make-up is from this city. I eventually graduated Trenton High School and began my college career at Rutgers University. There I started another rap group, began a successful DJ career and started one of the biggest Hip-Hop media companies in the world.....

......TO BE CONTINUED........

THE
TEN
HUSTLE
COMMANDMENTS

I. Persistence

Let's say you are a college freshman majoring in Theater Arts. One day you're in the counselor's office to discuss your future. Your counselor tells you that you will spend the next 6 years trying to get out of college. After college, you will spend the next 20 years traveling from state to state trying to find work. After suffering from a number of major setbacks, including a life-threatening drug addiction, you will finally get your big break exactly 21 years from your graduation date. After hearing this story from your counselor would you immediately change your major? Or will you continue with your dream?

Ok, maybe that one is a no-brainer. What about this one?

Let's say that you are a good cook. You have dreams of becoming a *great* cook and opening a few restaurants. You're 18 years old and your mother sits you down one day to discuss your future. She tells you that over the next 22 years you will try to sell your idea of a new restaurant to a number of existing business owners. On your way to chasing your dream, you will work as a firefighter, a steamboat driver, an insurance salesman and a gas station attendant just to make ends meet. Finally, at 40 years of age, you will decide to get in your car and travel from state to state cooking for different restaurants to show them your secret recipe. Finally after 12 years on the road, you will get your big break and a major investor will come on board to open your new restaurant chain. Now at 52, you will become one of the most powerful chefs in the country. After hearing this story from your mother, will you throw out all of your cookbooks and start thinking about college? Or will you continue with your dream?

Ok, you're right. That's too extreme. How about this one? Let's say that you are into sports. You feel that you're a good football player and you want to go to the NFL. So one day your high school coach sits you down to discuss your future. He tells you that the only way you can make it to the NFL is if you spend the next 3 years playing high school football and the next 4 years playing college football. And finally you must spend an additional 5 years playing football in Canada. And at 28 years of age you will finally be able to play in the NFL. After hearing this story from your coach, would you make the 12-year commitment? Or would you hit the books very hard and think about another line of work?

For Samuel L. Jackson, Colonel Harland Sanders and Warren Moon these three scenarios are all too real. How does an individual strive to become the highest grossing male actor of all time? How does a human being endure over 40 years of rejection to open the 3rd largest fast food restaurant in the world? What makes a man take a 5-year detour to realize his dream? Persistence!

Persistence is your ability to withstand the punishment and endure the hardships of the tough road to success. Just like there is no limit to the amount of success that one may experience in a lifetime, the same rings true for the amount of obstacles that one will encounter on the road to success.

Imagine your dream is on the top of a mountain. If the road to your dream is smooth with no ridges or sharp edges, the chances of you making it to your dream are slim to none. You need the rough edges, bumps and ridges to hold on to and overcome so that you can make your way to the top where your dream is waiting.

As you move closer and closer to your goal, you must realize that big dreams require a big heart. You must have more courage and more tenacity than the average human being. Storms will come and go; rough times will rise and subside. But the feeling of a dream realized is worth the ride.

II. Protect Your Dream

On your way to pursuing your dream, don't forget to protect yourself and your ideas at all times. How many times have you heard one of your friends, family members or co-workers tell you: "I saw something on TV that looks exactly like my idea! I can't believe they stole that idea from me!"? Or these same people see a product for sale and say; "I could have done that. I was just waiting to put it out there!"

The road to success is filled with scores of people who can tell you war stories about how they had good ideas that were taken from them. In most instances, these ideas were very innovative and, more importantly, have made someone else a lot of money.

No matter what industry you are currently working in, the concept of protection is very important and shouldn't be taken lightly. The biggest misconception about ideas and new "concepts" is that they are difficult to protect. This is so far from the truth. There are 3 levels of protection that you can use that will ensure that your ideas stay with you until you want to share them with the world. First you must protect yourself personally. Next you must protect yourself legally. And finally, protect yourself from viruses.

To explain this concept of protection further, I want to start a new business with you. You and I are going to develop a new concept right here, right now! Don't worry, it will be fun and won't cost you any money (in the physical form of course). I'm going to come up with the idea. I need you to follow the steps that I will give you in order to protect it. After this exercise you can take this blueprint and put it to use in any situation you wish.

The other day I was watching TV and thought to myself, "where the hell is the remote control? I hate when I do that!" Then the idea hit me. What if there was a way to never lose your remote control again? And then I developed the concept called "Remote Finder". Remote Finder is a 2way paging system that finds your lost remote when you are in need. The concept is simple; in fact, it is only two small pieces about the size of a quarter. The first piece is the pager that is placed on the remote control using double-sided tape. The other piece is the locater and is to be placed on the side of your television. If you lose the remote, just press the locator button on the side of your TV and a beeping noise will come from the pager located on the remote. The beeping will continue until you find the remote and disarm the system.

Now that you know the concept it is time to get to work.

Personal Protection

The first step in protecting this idea is to protect it "personally". The best way to personally protect this idea is to keep a "log" of the creative process. In order to do this, you must keep an accurate account of the dates and times in which we develop this concept. For instance, if I should call you in the near future and explain additional components of this idea, it is best that you jot down some notes, notate the date and time of the interaction and sign the entry. Every month send a copy of the "information" to yourself using your local post office. For additional insurance, send the package using certified mail and make sure you request a signature for delivery. The US Postal Service uses a timestamp system, so once the package is mailed a paper trail will be created.

This step is the least difficult and does not require much money. In fact, you may have heard this process referred to as "the poor man's copyright". Do not open the package for any reason unless you encounter a dispute over the ownership of the idea. If the package is not opened or tampered with, it will be eligible for use in a court of law. Please remember to include the name of the idea and the owner's information in every package to ensure proper documentation. Videotaping sessions and using audio equipment to record the creative process is also a good idea. Videotapes can play a crucial role in determining the true owners of this brilliant yet potentially lucrative idea.

Legal Protection

The next step to protecting this idea is to protect it "on paper". This is the most intricate of all the steps. You must take this step seriously because this is where the idea becomes legally yours.

Because this idea has a physical component to it, the very first step requires that you patent the idea. Patent protection is used when an idea serves as an invention. Because this new idea of the Remote Finder is a new invention, in order to protect this idea, you must file for a patent. The safest way to secure the patent for this idea would be to contact a credible patent attorney. Basic fees for patent attorneys can range from $200-$5,000. But don't let this number scare you. Most inventions are very basic in nature and will not require a lot of red tape. Once you secure the patent attorney, give the attorney the description of the invention as best as you can describe it. The patent attorney will first do a search to find out if there are any conflicting ideas. You can also conduct a simple search of the idea by logging onto the U.S. Patent Offices' website. The web address is http://www.uspto.gov. After the successful patent search, the entire process will take about 3-6 weeks for the patent to be certified.

Now before you kick your feet back and take a break, we must now "trademark" the name of the invention. The name of the invention is Remote Finder. I like this name because it is simple and easy to remember. Although the process to trademark the name is similar to the patent process, they both serve a different purpose. The patent protects "the way" in which an idea works. A trademark protects the actual "name" and "picture" of the logo.

I have decided that the logo for the Remote Finder will be a huge magnifying glass hovering over a small remote control with the words "Remote Finder" under it. This will be my trademark. I will locate a graphic designer to put the logo together for me and send you the picture. Once you get the picture you have to either log onto the Trademark Offices' website (http://www.uspto.gov) and conduct a search of the trademarks or contact a trademark attorney. It will be more cost-effective to research the information yourself. The process is simple and the website is easy to navigate. The basic filing fee for the trademark is $325. If you were to use a trademark attorney, you can pay upwards to $4,000 for one trademark. The entire trademark process can take up to 3 weeks to complete. Once the trademark is secured no one will be able to use the logo without legal ramifications.

Now that the patent is completed and the trademark is secured, I have now decided to write-up a small pamphlet that will explain what the Remote Finder is all about. The booklet will be about 8 pages in length and I will write all of the information in it. However, neither a patent nor a trademark will protect this work. I will need you to get copyright protection for this pamphlet. The copyright process is important here to protect the words that I write. Copyright is a form of protection provided by the laws of the United States to the authors of "original works of authorship," including literary, dramatic, musical, artistic, and other intellectual works. Once the booklet is complete, you will then mail the work, a copyright application and a $30 check to the Library of Congress /Copyright Office / Publications Section, LM-455/101 Independence Avenue, S.E./Washington, D.C. 20559-6000. You can also log on to http://www.copyright.gov and complete the information online. This process can take up to 2 months.

Other ways we can protect this idea legally is by securing a website. The domain name (or the name of the website) would be useful here. Once the domain name is secured, the creation date will show an interest in the idea for the rightful owners by setting up an online presence. A website can range from $99-$2000 to set up. Domain names are simple to obtain and can be secured easily at http://www.ultimatemediahosting.com.

Virus Protection

The last level of protection for this dream is the protection against the viruses.

In this example, these types of viruses have nothing to do with a common cold or a malfunctioning computer. Viruses are "people" in your immediate circle that are there to attack your dream. The medical term for a virus is an organism that attacks your body and deteriorates your physical condition. My definition for a virus is an organism that attacks your "mind" and deteriorates your mental condition. How many times have you heard that you can't do something or you won't succeed at a task? Now ask yourself how many times you have actually succeeded *despite* these failed attempts of discouragement. Viruses will continue to come in and out of your life and disrupt your path to success. However you must be strong in your position to succeed despite the noise. The closer the "virus" is to you, the harder it will be to disregard them. There is an old saying that states; "sometimes the most expensive advice is free advice". This simply means that if you take the advice of a person who is not knowledgeable or does not have your best interest in mind, you may pay for that advice your whole life. Remember to protect your dream at all times.

Now that we have reviewed all three levels of protection you are ready to continue on your path to success. Although the example of the Remote Finder is fictitious, your dreams and aspirations are very real and should be taken seriously. Remember that you are the master of your own destiny and protecting your dreams play an important part in pursuing them.

III. Keep It Legal

In the U.S., there are more than 2.1 million Americans incarcerated in state and federal prisons and local jails. This is the highest population ever recorded in the history of the United States, and represents a one-quarter increase in the US inmate population since 1995. Among black males age 25 to 29, approximately 13 percent were in prison or in jail, compared to less than 2 percent of white males in their late twenties. Overall, one in every 138 US residents are in prison or jail. Authors of the annual Crime and Punishment reports cite mandatory drug sentences as one of the primary reasons for the sharp increase in the US inmate population over the past decade.

So why am I giving you a lesson on the American prison system? It is important to understand that there are no shortcuts when it comes to reaching your dream. Many people mistake the term "hustle" as some kind of illegal activity. This is a gross misconception. The key to attaining your goals and realizing your dreams is the complete opposite. You must keep a level head and avoid all types of illegal activity.

I had a childhood friend name Darryle. We went to junior high school together. Darryle wasn't quiet or shy about anything that he wanted. We both were in the Gifted and Talented program and I always thought that he was smarter than I was. I remember Darryle telling me on a number of occasions that he wanted to play football and go to school to study medicine. It was so crazy because he was only 14 talking about trying to become a doctor. His grades were always A's with a few B's. He was very good in sports and eventually he went on to play football for our high school when we graduated.

Once we got to high school, Darryle did not stop pounding out those good grades and his name stayed in the local newspaper for his football skills. Towards junior year, Darryle and I started to spend less time together. I was still trying to pursue my hip-hop aspirations and Darryle started spending a lot of time at football camps and college prep courses.

After graduation, Darryle got accepted to play football for a Big East team down in North Carolina and I went off to college in New Jersey. I started to see his name pop up in some of the box scores on ESPN Sportscenter. I was definitely proud of him.

About a year later while I was back home visiting I picked up a newspaper to catch up on what was going on in my old neighborhood. I was flipping through the sports section expecting to read about my childhood friend doing well on the football field.

Instead, Darryle was on page 9 of the Trenton Times. Darryle had more hobbies than just playing sports and hitting the books. Darryle was arrested for drug possession with the intent to distribute. Over the next 18 months, Darryle had to endure a long trial that detailed how he was selling drugs on his college campus and making trips to the west coast to buy more drugs to sell. He was sentenced to 7 years in a federal prison.

Darryle was released from prison 4 years later for good behavior. Darryle lost his scholarship and was expelled from the school. He had to start his life all over again.

I saw Darryle about a year ago and he was trying to put things back together. He felt bad about how his life turned out and decided to speak to kids about the dangers of drug dealing. He said that because of his time in prison, his drive to become a doctor has since dwindled. He is planning to open a restaurant and wants to expand in different markets across the country.

Darryle is a smart guy and I would put my money on the fact that he will eventually open his restaurant and will be a successful business owner. Like I said, I always knew that he was smarter than me he just made a few bad mistakes.

I am convinced that at some point in your quest to become successful and realize your dream, you will be confronted with a situation that will challenge your integrity. It is at this point where you will make a decision that could affect your entire life. If you make the wrong decision you could easily pay the price of losing your dream as Darryle did. Doing things by the book will always prove to be a tougher road. But as you move closer and closer to your dream, building your foundation on the basis of the utmost integrity will prove to be the best decision. Other people will see a better person in you and will want to assist you on your way to the top.

IV. TeamWork

One of the biggest mistakes that one could make on the road to success is to try to travel it alone. Not only is it a selfish way to chase your dream but it is also risky. Some of the most successful icons of our time from Bill Cosby to Oprah Winfrey to Bill Clinton to Spike Lee to Russell Simmons all have knowledgeable individuals that they call on to answer tough questions and help support them as they work to overcome incredible obstacles.

The key to putting together a productive "Dream Team" is to be honest about your own personal shortcomings. For example, let's say that you're a very creative individual but you lack financial knowledge. This is a very realistic weakness and is nothing to be embarrassed about. The best way to combat this problem is to surround yourself with individuals who are strong in this area. Accountants, financial planners, loan officers or individuals who study financial knowledge are all likely candidates. These people will help you with questions that you may have in order to help you along your path.

Again, the key is to be honest with yourself and identify your weaknesses. Once the weaknesses are identified it is time to put your team together. There are a few rules to consider before you put your team together.

Rule #1: Make sure that every person that you consider to be a "teammate" understands your vision and understands your dream. Whether it is your business partner, your family member, friend, classmate or co-worker; if you have a specific goal in mind, you have to ensure that everyone is on the same page. Moving in unison towards a common goal is easier than moving in separate directions. Have weekly meetings and "brainstorming sessions" to make sure everyone is on the same page. There is nothing worse than trying to reach a goal and the process gets delayed due to a lack of continuity. These problems are very easy to fix in most cases with a little communication. This brings me to my next rule.

Rule #2: Always keep the lines of communication open. Information is more powerful than money in today's society. An exchange of ideas can make the difference between a team that merely competes and a team that wins. Take a look at the 2003-2004 Los Angeles Lakers for the best example. With the two most dominant players in the National Basketball Association, the L.A. Lakers still lost the 7-Game Championship Series against the Detroit Pistons just because of Shaquille O'Neal and Kobe

Bryant's lack of communication. Having meetings, sit-downs and sessions are all good ideas in keeping the lines of communication open. In fact, I recommend having at least one meeting per week with your "teammates".

Rule #3: Identify the viruses on your team and make changes. Every organization, team, corporate office, church group and company has a virus in it just waiting to rear its ugly head. Sometimes an individual that you feel is totally committed to the fight turns out to become vulnerable to this type of negative thinking. There are two ways that you can deal with the situation. You can totally remove this person from your circle or you can have a few meetings with the individual. If you notice that there is no change in his/her behavior you must exclude them from any future plans. You have to take your dream serious and eliminate all possible threats to its survival. In other words, don't let someone destroy the chances that you have to be successful.

Rule #4: Be honest with your team and challenge your team to be honest with you. This is the final but most important rule. Honesty and integrity begins at the core of your organization, which is made up of yourself and your team.

Now that we have reviewed the four most important rules in building your team, it is now time for you to continue on your path to success.

V. Think BIG

One of the most profound analogies that I have ever heard is that "life is like a flowing stream. Some people go to the stream for water and take a small cup, while some go to the stream with a barrel. And some people even learn how to pump water out of the stream for endless use".

I always found this analogy to be so powerful because I know dozens of people who lack the ability to Think BIG. I have even found myself, on a number of occasions, thinking small and not pushing the limits. It goes back to the old proverb that states, "You have not" because "you ask not".

There is more wealth in the world today than any other period in the history of the modern world. According to a study conducted by the United Nations in 2003, 225 of the richest individuals in the world account for a little over $1 trillion of the world's wealth. Not Billion! Trillion! To understand the scope of this number let me write it out for you; $1,000,000,000,000. In fact, these same 225 people have more money than the annual income of the 2.5 billion poorest people on earth. Please take a moment to think about that fact. There are a little over 5 billion people on the planet earth. And only 225 people have more money than what ½ of the population makes in a year. That is an amazing fact! Microsoft CEO Bill Gates has more wealth than the bottom 45% of the U.S. population combined. So why am I giving you a lesson on wealth? In order to gain great wealth and accomplish great things, you have to think larger than the average person.

The sad fact is that most people are content with leading a mediocre life and they settle for just getting by. And then there are other people that are so insecure about the things they can achieve and the obstacles they can overcome. I personally trace this insecurity back to childhood. When we were children, our parents, teachers and older family members continuously scolded us about the things we "cannot" do. How many times does a child hear: "don't touch that", "stop", "don't go down there" or even the infamous "sit down somewhere and be quiet"? It is not that our parents, teachers and older family members are bad people. And although they mean well, this continuous barrage of negative commands condition our minds to always be weary about the things we can and cannot do. As a result, when we set out to do things we *think* that we *can* accomplish. But in order to accomplish things that are even greater than our very own existence, we must think bigger and believe that we can accomplish things way beyond the scope of reality.

So how does one Think BIG?

There are a few exercises that you can do to condition your mind to Think BIG. One step you can take is to unlearn all those negative commands that suggest that you can't do something. Every major accomplishment in the world, from the construction of the great pyramids in Egypt, to landing on the moon to the development of the Internet has all started with the same occurrence. An Idea! Every stable mind has the ability to create and develop an idea. When an idea hits you and you begin to hear that voice that tries to discourage you, you must disregard it and continue with the process. No matter how silly or far-fetched the idea may seem, simply write out the details and begin to develop the idea. If you believe in the idea, make the idea bigger and bigger until it is something that the world has never seen before.

Another step you can take in order to Think BIG is to avoid getting in the way of your own ideas. This is an important step. How many ideas have hit you when you didn't have the proper information or the proper background to thoroughly pursue it? If you find yourself developing ideas outside of your area of expertise don't get discouraged. This simply means that you must consider recruiting a "Dream Team" to assist with the efforts. Don't let your limitations or your lack of information stifle your ability to develop great ideas.

The bigger the idea, the harder the road will be. On your road to success, thinking BIG is very important. The world is filled with limitless possibilities. It is up to you to take your barrel down to the stream of life and take what you need to accomplish your goals.

VI. Blood In, Blood Out

Family is always an interesting topic that arises on the road to success. Most people say that you can't mix family and business. I happen to agree with most people. However, I am a person that works with my family continuously on my various projects. There are a number of pros and cons that you must keep in mind if you decide to include your family in your plans for success.

First, we will review the negative side to dealing with your family. Let me pose a question to you. Do you believe that it is easier to convince your family or a total stranger that you will be successful? For some people, the answer would be "a total stranger". But if you grew up under similar circumstances as I, you will immediately say "your family". Why do you think this is so? Most of your family members may suffer from a condition that my business partner likes to call the "retail syndrome".

This simply means that your family only sees you for your retail value or the value that you have today. The longer your family member is around you, the more they will see you in terms of your retail value. However, a total stranger may see your passion and drive from an unbiased perspective and believe in you more. If your family suffers from this condition, convincing them that you will be successful might be a difficult task. This may also create problems if you decide to work with them. You can easily combat this problem by leading by example. As you make progress and move closer and closer to your goals, your family will have no choice but to take notice and realize that your goals will be attained.

Another pitfall that you have to watch for while working with your family is the tendencies and effects of emotional attachment. If you are working with your family to reach a certain goal, it is very possible that you will overlook certain mistakes or shortcomings due to your emotional attachment to that person. This emotional attachment can also bring about another problem. Instead of overlooking mistakes and shortcomings you may over-scrutinize and hold your family to a higher standard because of the emotional ties. Both issues are equally problematic. The key here is to stay focused on the goal and maintain a workable balance. While working with your family, you must find a way to separate the emotional attachment from the work environment. This is not an easy task and every situation is totally different. The goal is to recognize the problems in the early stages and correct them before they escalate.

Now that we have reviewed the negative side of working with your family, lets move on to the positive side. Working with family members can bring a sense of trust and integrity to your business. Wal-Mart, Ford Motor, The New York Times, Mars Incorporated, The Washington Post and Mary Kay are all examples of family owned businesses. Most entrepreneurs credit the success of the business to the fact that they are able to trust and communicate with their business partners. In my personal experience, working with family has given me a sense of community and the ability to help my family prosper.

VII. Do Your Homework

On March 20, 2003 The United States of America launched the largest military strike against the country of Iraq in US history. The principle rationale for the War in Iraq was the refusal of the then Iraqi president Saddam Hussein to destroy the weapons of mass destruction that his country allegedly possessed. On the recommendations of the State Department led by Colin Powell, the U.S. waged one of the bloodiest wars in recent U.S. history. After more than two years of fighting and the deaths of thousands of American troops, no trace was ever found of the disputed weapons of mass destruction. George Bush, the American president at the time, found himself losing approval ratings and answering tough questions about the validity of the war. How could this happen? How could a country wage war based on false information? The answer is simple. Someone forgot to do their homework.

Throughout school we have been given one of the most important tools for success nearly every day. Homework. Homework is what makes the mind sharp and keeps us informed of things that are going on around us. In school, we were given homework for math and science. It's no different in the business world. We just have more subjects to cover. No matter what your dream is or what your idea of success may be, it is important to research individuals, events, trends and other important factors that pertain to your industry. Here are a few resources you can use to keep up with your homework.

The fastest way to get information today is also the cheapest way to get information. Of course I am speaking of the Internet. I am personally a contributor of the online industry and have found the Internet to be very useful. Many people from our parents' generation and even older people frown upon the Internet and question its validity. However, the Internet has proven to be a great resource for information including accurate dates and facts on the spot. In fact, when it comes to news on certain topics, websites tend to get the news even before the traditional media outlets including television and magazines. There is one major problem with the Internet, however. Because of the large number of competing websites, I suggest researching a number of different information outlets, instead of basing your decisions on one source. Double check and triple check your facts to make sure you are getting the proper information.

Another way to get information and the latest updates on what's going on in your industry is to build a network of reliable sources. Having a friend, colleague or co-worker that you can depend on for information is always helpful. Networking parties and conventions are great places to meet new contacts and sources. Keep in mind that this information is usually free but also comes from a third party. So research and fact checking is very important when using third party sources.

The most reliable way to get information is by "beating the pavement". You have to get out there and witness it for yourself. You must hit the bookstores and obtain researched and proven information about your industry. You must contact the heavy hitters and major players in your field. You must attend conferences, seminars, meetings and other engagements to witness how people in your industry made things happen. These are the things you have to add to your list of homework to do.

While gathering information and researching your industry, it is important to look for the most intricate facts about your business. Make sure you know who the major players are in your industry and everything about them. How long did it take for them to be successful? What are some of the horror stories that they have about your industry? What schools did they attend? You need to know what type of money is in the industry that you want to pursue. How much did your industry gross last year? What are the current financial trends in the industry? You want to find out if someone else has tried your idea. And if so, how can you improve on it? Other things to look for are the legal issues associated with your industry. What are the potential legal pitfalls that you may encounter on your path? And what are some of the ways to bypass them? You also have to research your competition. Whether you are trying to start a business or you are doing a solo mission, your competition must be identified and researched. Is your competition a major threat to your idea or dream? What kinds of problems are they having with their own journey? How could you improve on *your* business or idea to surpass theirs?

The research on your industry has to be so thorough that you can layout a 5-year plan without a hitch. The one thing to remember about doing homework is that it never ends. Homework is what keeps Fortune 500 companies ahead of the competition. Corporate spies are dispatched everyday to find out what the other side is up to. As you move ahead on your path to success you will realize that <u>every</u> advantage needs to be taken very seriously and exploited to stay ahead.

For most people, doing homework was very difficult because they could not see the purpose in doing it. Most people felt they should be excluded from homework if they understood the lessons. But the real jewel in doing homework is to keep your mind in the game. It serves as a reminder that there is a bigger goal to accomplish. It is also important to make sure that your Dream Team is also involved in the process. Giving homework to your team is also a good way to keep them sharp and current on your industry. Keep in mind that information is power.

VIII. Share The Wealth

As you move closer and closer to your goals you will begin to reap the benefits of your intense labor and hard work. The more successful you become the more generous you should become. Many people say, "The quickest way to make money is to save money". Although this statement is valid, being selfish is never a good business practice. It is important to those in your organization, group or team to feel appreciated. Of course, the best way for your teammates to feel appreciated is through monetary compensation. However, there are additional ways to show your teammates that you appreciate them.

Getting your teammates more involved with your creative process is one way for you to share the wealth of your organization. Not only is this a good way to keep the lines of communication open, but it's a good way to send a message to your team that you value their input. In this example, you should never be selfish with the creative process.

No matter what industry you are striving to excel in, once your success reaches a certain level you will begin to draw media attention. Here is an opportunity to give back to your Dream Team. When you get a call to conduct an interview for a local newspaper or television show, ask your team members to tag along to share in the glory. This sends a message to the outside world that you have serious thinkers behind your project. It also shows your team that you value their effort and hard work. In this example, you should never be selfish with the spotlight.

Another strategy you can use to show your team that you appreciate them is by creating a new business. Most successful companies are good at spawning new companies. For example, when The Google Search Engine Company found itself getting larger and larger the CEO decided to offer free email. This spawned a new company called Gmail. A number of executives from the search engine immediately moved over to the Gmail division, which gave them more responsibility and higher salaries. Although your company or organization is not on the Google level, branching out and developing new ideas will give your teammates additional avenues to shine and prosper. Keeping an open mind about new projects is important here. In this example you should never be selfish with your ideas.

Most ideas come to us when we are alone. As we develop the idea and our dreams become larger and larger, more people are added to our Dream Team. It is important to share the wealth both monetarily and creatively.   Remember, there is enough to go around for everyone.

VIIII. Your Word Is Law

It was stated previously in this book that everything unnatural in this world started as an idea. Next to an idea, the second most powerful force in the creative process is your word. Words are the fuel of this modern world that we live in. Words help dictate how big an idea can become. Words help communicate to others the scope of your idea. Words help navigate your team and coordinate your resources to help accomplish your goals. Because your word is law in your own personal universe, it is very important that you monitor the way you communicate with yourself and with others.

Let's do a quick experiment. I want you to think of a person that you continue to do business with because of their honesty. Now I want you to think of a person you don't do business with anymore because of their dishonesty. Who came to mind faster? 9 times out of 10 you will identify the dishonest person faster. This is because as human beings, negative situations tend to make more of an impression on our lives. Therefore, as a dishonest person, or a person who can't be taken at his or her word, you will always be remembered as someone who cannot be counted on. This is never good for business.

In most cases, especially with small companies, your word is the only credit and insurance that others can rely on while doing business with you. It doesn't matter if you are trying to create a new product or start a major corporation, your word will become your calling card throughout your industry. Being on time for meetings, delivering products on schedule, paying your bills on time and meeting important deadlines are all key factors in keeping your word. If you are the type of business person that keeps your word, your reputation will spread. If you are the type of business person that doesn't keep your word, your reputation will spread...much faster! It is important that you take every business interaction serious and build a good resume for yourself. Word of mouth can be your biggest asset or liability when you are trying to get a project off the ground.

There is one person, in particular, that you must communicate with carefully. Yourself. Talking to yourself and giving yourself advice is a natural occurrence, especially for individuals trying to accomplish major things. The words you use to push yourself are very important. Because your word is law, it is important to give yourself positive reinforcement. Don't talk down to yourself or punish yourself for not accomplishing a specific goal. Simply learn from your mistakes and move forward.

Ironically, as you move closer and closer to your goals, you will become your very own first line of defense. Your confidence, drive and persistence will come from within initially. One strategy you can use to keep your spirits up is by writing positive statements about yourself on a small piece of paper. Keep it on your person as you travel about. When things become rough and you begin to feel discouraged, refer back to the statements and put yourself back on track. Remember, your ideas create the spark but your words keep the fire burning. Choose them wisely and live by them.

X. Keep The Faith

There comes a time in everyone's life when the faith in yourself and your ability will be tested. You may find yourself suffering setback after setback with no good news in sight. It may come a time when you find yourself running out of resources and questioning your decisions. It is at this time when you have to dig deeper and believe in yourself. There are no magic pills, no seminars or books that can teach you how to keep the faith. Everyone is born with it and tapping into it is a personal journey. You know exactly what you want out of life. What you don't know is that you can reach your goals within this lifetime if you simply believe in yourself.

-order more copies of-

FROM POVERTY TO POWER MOVES

Full Name _____

(street address)

(City)   (State)   (Zip Code)

(Check All That Applies to you)
☐ Avid Reader ☐ Church Leader

(Phone Number) "optional"
☐ Student ☐ Book Club ☐ Distributor

☐ Teacher ☐ Inmate ☐ Author

(Email Address)

─── PRICING INFO ───

☐ 1-10 Books ($14.95/Book)

☐ 11-100 Books ($10.95/Book)

☐ 101-500 Books ($8.95/Book)

I Would Like To Order _____ Book(s)
(Amount)

: : : : FREE SHIPPING ON ALL BOOK ORDERS : : : :

Special Instructions (Schools, Correctional Facilities And/Or Churches)

_____

_____

_____

Please Send Your Check Or Money Order To:

Dashawn Taylor
c/o POWER MOVES
PO Box 8644
Newark, NJ 07108

"PLEASE ALLOW 5-7 BUSINESS DAYS FOR SHIPPING WITHIN THE USA"

"TRUST NO ONE"

KISSED BY THE DEVIL

THE NEW
"URBAN THRILLER"
BY

DASHAWN TAYLOR

IN STORES NOW

WWW.KISSEDBYTHEDEVIL.COM